D1526754

Sponsored by
The International Academy of Education

The general aim of the Academy is to foster scholarly excellence in all fields of education. Towards this end, the Academy's goals are:

- To create an international network of scholars to write state-of-the-art reports on major educational issues, to establish permanent relations among relevant disciplines of education, and to identify excellent practices wherever they might be found
- To disseminate knowledge about effective policies and practices to interested educators
- To conduct advanced training, particularly seminars for education officials, research workers, and other key staff
- To provide critical and evaluative perspectives on studies and issues in the forefront of educational debate
- To identify research priorities relating to critical issues in education
- To strengthen communication and cooperation between educational researchers and educational practitioners
- To award an annual prize for distinguished contributors to educational scholarship

THE HOME ENVIRONMENT
AND
SCHOOL LEARNING

Thomas Kellaghan
Kathryn Sloane
Benjamin Alvarez
Benjamin S. Bloom

THE HOME ENVIRONMENT
AND
 # SCHOOL LEARNING

Promoting Parental Involvement
in the
Education of Children

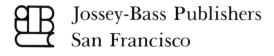 Jossey-Bass Publishers
San Francisco

Substantial discounts on bulk quantities of Jossey-Bass books are available to corporations, professional associations, and other organizations. For details and discount information, contact the special sales department at Jossey-Bass Inc., Publishers. (415) 433-1740; Fax (415) 433-0499.

For sales outside the United States, contact Maxwell Macmillan International Publishing Group, 866 Third Avenue, New York, New York 10022.

Manufactured in the United States of America

The paper used in this book is acid-free and meets the State of California requirements for recycled paper (50 percent recycled waste, including 10 percent postconsumer waste), which are the strictest guidelines for recycled paper currently in use in the United States.

10% POST CONSUMER WASTE

The ink in this book is either soy- or vegetable-based and during the printing process emits fewer than half the volatile organic compounds (VOCs) emitted by petroleum-based ink.

Library of Congress Cataloging-in-Publication Data

The home environment and school learning : promoting parental involvement in the education of children / Thomas Kellaghan . . . [et al.]. — 1st ed.
        p.   cm. — (The Jossey-Bass education series)
    Includes bibliographical references (p.   ) and index.
    ISBN 1-55542-588-7 (alk. paper)
    1. Home and school.   2. Education—Parent participation.
I. Kellaghan, Thomas.   II. Series.
LC225.H645   1993
649'.68—dc20   93-14552
                                                                           CIP

FIRST EDITION
HB Printing   10 9 8 7 6 5 4 3 2 1   *Code 9387*

■ THE JOSSEY-BASS
EDUCATION SERIES

◼ CONTENTS

◼ PREFACE

Although the important role that the home plays in children's school learning has long been recognized, recent years have seen a surge in the development of programs designed to increase families' involvement in their children's education. A number of reasons can be advanced for this activity. First, the cumulative impact of research findings has been to underline the importance of the home in contributing to children's school progress, at times even suggesting that the home may be more important than the school. Second, reform efforts that focused on the school to improve student retention rates and achievement, such as the provision of new curricula and materials, have not been as successful as had been hoped, prompting policy makers to look elsewhere for ways to improve student learning. Third, a review of radical changes in the structure and function of families gives rise to concern about families' ability under pressures of varying kinds to provide the conditions that foster children's scholastic development.

If one sets out to design or select a program to increase parent involvement, one has to address the basic question: what are the best means to achieve this goal? Choice of means will obviously be influenced by an assessment of the needs and circumstances of the families that the program will serve. A further consideration, however, should be the findings of research on the conditions of homes that promote scholastic development.

It is the latter consideration that this book addresses. We asked whether the available research on home-school relations could provide us with sufficient information to design a program for action in homes that parents could use to support and improve children's school learning. Our search of the literature indicated that although research still leaves many questions unanswered it had gone a long way in identifying the characteristics of homes that are closely associated with children's progress at school. On the basis of that information, as well as of evidence on the effects of parent involvement programs, we present the outline of a program that we believe can be effective in helping parents promote the educational development of their children. There is already some empirical evidence that the program can have an impact on a variety of home and parent characteristics, as well as on children's school achievement. The program may be used on its own, although in the light of current thinking on parent involvement, it is more likely to be incorporated into a larger program designed to improve home-school relations or increase parents' participation in their children's education.

We believe that the review of research on the role of the home in children's education and the program for parent involvement presented in this book will be of interest to parents, teachers, and other educators who see the need to develop the potential of homes to support children's education. It should also be of interest to policy makers and planners in education as well as to students preparing to be teachers.

In Chapter One, we consider evidence that, while acknowledging the important role of schools, suggests that on their own schools are not likely to be able to deal with all children's educational problems. We also consider evidence that underlines the key role the home has to play if children's educational development is to be satisfactory. In Chapter Two, we consider reasons why homes and schools do not always play the complementary and mutually reinforcing roles one might expect in children's education; we also look at a variety of efforts being made throughout the world to get homes and schools to work in unison.

In Chapters Three and Four, we review research findings on relationships between home backgrounds and school learning. Although studies that used fairly crude indices of family conditions, such as socioeconomic status and family structure, have found these variables to be related to school learning, the relationships are not strong. Studies that have described what parents do in the home, rather than what their home status is, have been much more successful in identifying the factors closely related to school success.

In Chapter Five, we outline some of the particular difficulties that changing societal and family circumstances are creating for parents who are trying to meet the educational needs of their children. While many families cope with these difficulties, others may require assistance from outside institutions, including the school, if they are to meet basic needs or improve the conditions required to support their children's learning.

In Chapter Six, we describe some of the efforts that have been made over the past three decades to help parents develop a home learning environment that will foster their children's cognitive abilities, school readiness skills, and learning at school. In Chapter Seven, a review of studies on the effects of programs to assist parents in their children's formal education leads to the conclusion that programs that help parents become stronger partners in their children's learning can have a significant and positive impact on children's cognitive development and school performance.

In Chapter Eight, we turn our attention to the cognitive and noncognitive characteristics of children that seem to underlie scholastic development and in the development of which the home plays a crucial role. Chapter Nine provides an outline of a program designed to help develop these characteristics, drawing on the research described in Chapter Four on the identification of aspects of the home environment that are closely related to the scholastic performance of children.

In Chapter Ten, we summarize the major findings of the research described earlier in the book, on the role of families in education, and consider the implications of the findings for parents' involvement in their children's education. Finally, we consider how a program based on the findings reported in this work might be used to improve home-school relationships.

The authors are indebted to the International Academy of Education, under whose auspices this book was prepared. The Academy, with funds provided by the John D. and Catherine T.

MacArthur Foundation, arranged for the authors of the book to meet on two occasions. A further meeting was held in which Academy members reacted to an earlier draft. The authors wish to express their gratitude to the following Academy members for their support throughout the life of the project: T. Neville Postlethwaite, Torsten Husén, Herbert J. Walberg, James S. Coleman, Gilbert De Landsheere, and Hellmut Becker. We are also indebted to Lesley Iura, Frank Welsch, and Christie Hakim of Jossey-Bass and to anonymous reviewers of an earlier version. Finally, we wish to thank Teresa Bell and Hilary Keenan, who typed the manuscript, and Muireann Joy, Mary Rohan, and Frank Byrne for editorial assistance.

August 1993   Thomas Kellaghan
                                       Dublin, Ireland

                                       Kathryn Sloane
                                       Berkeley, California

                                       Benjamin Alvarez
                                       Battle Creek, Michigan

                                       Benjamin S. Bloom
                                       Chicago, Illinois

■ THE AUTHORS

Thomas Kellaghan is director of the Eduational Research⋅ Centre at St. Patrick's College in Dublin, Ireland. He received his B.A. degree (1959) and his Ph.D. degree (1965) from Queen's University, Belfast, Northern Ireland, in psychology, and has taught at that university and at the University of Ibadan, Nigeria. His research interests relate to educational assessment and factors that influence scholastic development. His books include *The Evaluation of an Intervention Programme for Disadvantaged Children* (1977), *The Effects of Standardized Testing* (with G. F. Madaus and P. W. Airasian, 1982), *Teach Them Well: An Introduction to Education* (with G. F. Madaus and R. L. Schwab, 1989), and *Transition Education in Irish Schools* (with M. Lewis, 1991).

Kathryn Sloane is research educator in the Graduate School of Education and program evaluator at the Lawrence Hall of Science, at the University of California, Berkeley. She received her B.A. degree (1976) from the College of Charleston in English literature and her M.Ed. degree (1979) from the University of South Carolina in educational research. She worked with Benjamin Bloom on the home environment component of the Development of Talent Project at the University of Chicago. She continues to study the home's influence on children's learning through methodological work on assessing home environmental processes and through evaluations of parent education programs. As a National Academy of Education Spencer Fellow, she is currently developing methodologies for examining congruence between home and school learning environments and the relative effects of the two environments on children's conceptions of and competencies in mathematics. Her publications include papers on home-school relationships and the development of talent.

Benjamin Alvarez is research and evaluation manager at the International Youth Foundation in Battle Creek, Michigan. He received his B.A. degree (1963) from the Universidad Javeriana, Bogotá, in philosophy. He earned his M.A. degree (1969) in education and psychology as well as the Ph.D. degree (1973) in education and social sciences from the University of New Mexico. He has taught at universities in Colombia and has been senior program officer in the Fellowships and Awards Division of the International Development Research Centre, Ottawa. His main research interests relate to human and educational development. Publications include *Ciencia, Educación Superior y Desarrollo en América Latina* (Science, higher education, and development in Latin America; 1991) and *Family and Learning: Readings from Recent Research* (with N. Iriarte, 1991).

Benjamin S. Bloom is emeritus distinguished service professor of education at the University of Chicago. He received his A.B. and M.S. degrees from Pennsylvania State College in psychology and his Ph.D. degree from the University of Chicago in education. For most of his life, he taught at the University of Chicago. His research interests are in evaluation, educational measurement, and human development. His books include *Taxonomy of Educational Objectives* (editor, 1956), *Stability and Change in Human Characteristics* (1964), *Handbook on Formative and Summative Evaluation of Student Learning* (with J. T. Hastings and G. F. Madaus, 1971), *Human Characteristics and School Learning* (1976), and *Developing Talent in Young People* (editor, 1985). Bloom was a founding member of the International Association for the Evaluation of Educational Achievement and a past president of the American Educational Research Association.

THE HOME ENVIRONMENT
AND
SCHOOL LEARNING

Home and School: ■ ONE
Institutions for
Child Development

In the present-day world, education (and in many cases the formal qualifications associated with it) may be considered essential for accessing most areas of life. If young people fail to acquire basic skills and information by the time they leave school, their prospects for employment and for participating fully in the social and cultural life of society are likely to be extremely limited.

Many people associate most learning and even adult success primarily with school. In fact, however, the home, and in Western society the media, especially television, are also major influences on children's development. Increasingly, a variety of factors in the community and neighborhood are also being recognized as important. These include parental employment, the institutions to which individuals have access, the social networks and agencies available in the neighborhood, and the cultural traditions from which the family draws its values, beliefs, and practices (Bronfenbrenner, 1986). Important though these factors may be, it is probably true to say that their effects on children's development are mediated primarily through their influence on the family.

The balance among the various influences on children's development varies in different societies and has varied during different historical periods. Today, the relative importance of home and school differs considerably in different parts of the

1

world. With universal schooling occupying longer and longer periods of young people's lives, the importance of the school in Western society has increased. However, there are still countries in which many children do not go to school at all, or go only for short periods, or are handicapped in learning because the language of instruction differs from the language of their homes. In these cases, home and community may continue to play the major role in children's acquisition of values, knowledge, and even work skills (Cummings, 1990). However, as participation in the educational system increases in these countries, the balance between the roles of home and school is changing. As more young people attend school and stay at school for longer periods of time, one would expect the relative influence of schools to increase.

Although high rates of school participation have already been achieved in Western societies, the balance between the roles of home and school appears again to be changing. Many factors contribute to this situation, the most important of which are the radical changes taking place in the nature and functioning of families. As we shall see in Chapter Five, these changes make it difficult for some families to play their traditional role in supporting children's educational development. This raises the question: will schools (and other agencies) have to provide a larger share of educational inputs or are there ways in which the role of families can be strengthened to help them in their educational tasks? We hope that the answer to this question will become clear as the reader moves through the book.

In this chapter, we begin by considering the growth that has taken place in the extent and importance of schooling over the last two centuries. Despite this growth, we shall see that concerns are still expressed about the effectiveness of schooling in dealing with problems of equity in society and in providing all children with the knowledge and skills that they will require to function in adult life. Although many school reforms have addressed these problems, their relative lack of success has focused attention on children's home backgrounds and on the role that families play in children's school learning. Evidence on the role of the family in the promotion of children's learning, which we will consider later in the chapter, points strongly to the conclusion that support from children's homes is essential if children are to be successful in school.

The Importance of Schooling

Although there is evidence that schooling for social elites flourished in several civilizations in the past (for example, in Sumerian cultures in Babylonia and in pre-Columbian cultures in Latin America), it is only relatively recently that whole populations of children started going to school. Up to the time of the Industrial Revolution, the home took major responsibility for care, education, and training of children. In the largely informal atmosphere of the home, children learned about the world, developed attitudes toward it, and acquired skills to deal with day-to-day tasks, including those of work. This was possible because the occupational skills that most young people had to learn were relatively simple, related to farming, hunting, fishing, housekeeping, and crafts. Boys learned the skills of their father, girls those of their mother.

The need for instruction outside the home became acute during the Industrial Revolution. With the diminution of the home's importance as an economic production unit, work moved out of the home and into the factory; at the same time, it became more specialized and skilled. As knowledge accumulated, the need arose for people to devote themselves full-time to the instruction of the young, who could no longer gain sufficient knowledge and skills simply by observing and participating in the work of their elders at home. Further, as the economy became more complex, large numbers of people moved from the countryside to work in centers of industry. Increases in industrialization and urbanization both served to underline the need for a special agency to deal with the preparation of children in society. When it became obvious that the family could no longer provide children with the skills they needed to fill the new positions in industry, communities came to accept education and training as their responsibilities. Over a period of a century and a half, the school became critical in the determination of people's lives, in terms of personal expectations, public policy and budget commitments, and in the overall development of human and economic resources.

A range of studies carried out in a variety of conditions provide evidence that schooling confers a variety of benefits, both for individuals and for society. Benefits to the individual include an increased likelihood of employment in urban labor markets, higher wage levels, greater productivity, and better health and nutritional status. Society benefits because, as research and experience indicate, an educated labor force is necessary for economic development. No country has achieved significant economic growth without first attaining universal primary education; and the most successful of the newly industrialized economies all achieved high enrollments in secondary school (Lockheed and Verspoor, 1991; Owen, 1988; Walberg, 1984).

At present, most six- to eleven-year-old children throughout the world are enrolled in some sort of primary school. Almost all industrialized societies reached the goal of universal basic education several decades ago; and since the 1950s, developing countries and international development agencies have made the expansion of schooling a major priority, for economic and social reasons. In Africa, for example, a growing political interest in making primary education universal was made explicit as far back as 1961 in a declaration by thirty-five ministers of education that formal education constituted a critical priority. At that time, only 16 percent of African children of school age were enrolled in school (Omari and others, 1983), a situation that has subsequently changed radically for most though not all of the continent.

In many parts of the world there is still room for improvement in primary school attendance, mainly among groups that have suffered discrimination in the past—indigenous populations, rural communities, those living in the slums of large cities, and females. Members of these groups tend to fail to enroll in the first place or, if they do enroll, show the highest dropout and repetition rates during schooling.

Despite the increasing availability of education and the expanding roles and functions of the school, many people have long been concerned about the quality of the education being provided. In many countries, there is a feeling that the level of achievement of some students and their preparation for the world of work are inadequate. It has been concluded that few schools in developing countries successfully provide students with basic competencies in numeracy, literacy, and the ability to apply basic skills to new problems (Lockheed and Verspoor, 1991). In the United States, international comparisons of student performance and a decline over time in performance on achievement tests, together with other indicators, motivated the publication of a report entitled *A Nation at Risk: The Imperative for Educational Reform* (National Commission on Excellence in Education, 1983), whose main purpose was to promote change in the educational system to improve its quality. Recent educational reform in the former Soviet Union reflected similar concerns, although it was less critical of the previous work of the educational system (Kondakov, 1987).

The World Conference on Education for All — which was convened jointly by the executive heads of the United Nations International Children's Emergency Fund (UNICEF), United Nations Development Programme (UNDP), the United Nations Educational, Scientific, and Cultural Organization (UNESCO), and the World Bank — adopted as its main concern problems relating to the quality of elementary education in countries across the world. In addition to attending to the needs of children who were falling outside the primary education network, it acknowledged the failure in many cases of school attendance to provide children with useful knowledge, reasoning ability, skills, and values, pointing out that effective educational strategies, not just enrollment in school programs, are required to deal with these problems (*World Declaration on Education for All and Framework for Action to Meet Basic Learning Needs,* 1990).

The Limitations of Schooling

Not only have the number of schools and the number of children attending them expanded dramatically during the second half of this century, but new and significant functions for schools are constantly being proposed in addition to their traditional functions of teaching mathematics, science, reading, and religious practice. These new functions include many that were carried out by other institutions in the past, such as forming good citizens, promoting independent and creative thinking, training for jobs, changing attitudes, maintaining cultural traditions, and developing political values. If that is not enough, schools are also expected to promote equality, diversity, and competition. Efforts made over recent decades to equip schools for these tasks include the reform of school curricula, the specification of minimum competencies for graduation, and the development of better relations between families and schools.

Since the school has been assigned the responsibility in society for the formal education of children and is given public funds to perform that task, it might be argued that it should deal with children's learning difficulties when they occur, whatever their source. Moll and Diaz (1987) have concluded on the basis of anthropological evidence "that success and failure is in the social organization of schooling, in the organization of the experience itself" (p. 311), while Silvern (1988) has argued that "rather than teaching parents how to teach their children, teachers should make a concerted effort to find out what the child does at home and to incorporate this into school activities" (p. 156). Aronowitz and Giroux (1988) made more explicit how this might be done when they proposed that schools should recognize the categories of meaning that students bring with them to the classroom, since it is in terms of these meanings, often ignored in the school curriculum, that students produce and interpret knowledge.

While not denying that schools have a crucial role in children's learning and in dealing with difficulties when they occur, experience to date would suggest that, on their own, schools are not likely to be totally successful in meeting all of society's expectations. There are a number of reasons for adopting this view.

First, even though major curricular reforms have been underway in many countries since the beginning of the 1970s, it would seem that few have achieved the goal of raising students' achievements substantially. Many commentators claim that the available evidence indicates that average achievement levels in reading comprehension, science, and mathematics fell in American schools through the 1970s. Although gains were apparent in the 1980s, pre-1970 standards have not been attained (Hoffer and Coleman, 1990).

Second, the recent history of schooling has taught us that the mere expansion of education does not necessarily lead to greater participation by people of lower socioeconomic status in the benefits of education or of society. Despite the fact that more students are staying at school for longer periods of time, children from lower socioeconomic homes continue to be underrepresented in higher education. Even when children perform at a similar level on a measure of general scholastic ability, those who come from homes of high socioeconomic status are more likely to go on to third-level education than students who come from homes of low socioeconomic status (Greaney and Kellaghan, 1984).

Third, efforts in many countries to distribute resources for schooling more equitably, from urban to rural settings or across social, economic, and cultural groups, have not been very successful. The result is that even within a single country, variance in school quality can be very large. This is particularly true in developing countries where research indicates that school resources play a more important role than in industrialized societies in explaining school performance (Heyneman and Loxley, 1983; Omari and others, 1983; Schiefelbein and Simons, 1981).

Fourth, in most developing countries, efforts to expand public education have been hampered by a lack of resources, trained teachers, and effective management systems. Because of lack of space, many children receive only a few years of primary school education, and this does not seem long enough to develop basic literacy and numeracy skills. Further, schools often lack textbooks, blackboards, and basic physical facilities (Lockheed and Verspoor, 1991).

Fifth, not only are resources limited, but in most countries, expenditure on public education did not grow during the 1980s at the same rate as in previous decades. The impact of the recent world economic recession has been especially marked in the developing countries, in many of which expenditure on education has actually decreased. For example, in African countries, despite an increase in the numbers enrolled in schools, the average percentage of gross national product spent on education fell from 5.5 to 4.3 between 1980 and 1983, while the average percentage of total government expenditure devoted to education decreased from 16.2 to 11.9 (World Bank, 1988, Table A-14). Such decreases in resources for child care and education are becoming widespread and are likely to have serious long-term effects (see Jolly and Cornia, 1984). That the situation is not going to change in the near future seems clear; it is unlikely that public school programs aimed at improving the conditions of preschool and primary school children will increase in number or improve in quality in most parts of the world. Given this situation, the choice for policy makers is stark. For at least the remainder of this century, that choice would appear to lie either in increased efficiency in the use of existing resources or in the acceptance of declining standards of access, equity, and scholastic achievement (Windham, 1986).

The limited success of school-based reform efforts, the fact that resources for formal education are inadequate in many countries, and the variety of needs of the present generation of students that must be met during their educational careers all point to the conclusion that we cannot rely on the school alone to prepare young people to cope with the demands of modern society. It seems most unlikely that a significant improvement in the quality of education of all students can be achieved without active support from other quarters. In recognition of this situation, a concern of much thinking on education in the last decade has been to determine how the school can share its responsibilities with other institutions, particularly families—a concern that has led to a resurgence in "reemphasizing the educative role of the family and assisting the home in functioning as an effective learning center" (Bobbitt and Paolucci, 1986, p. 48).

Reasons for Home Involvement

There are several reasons—some intuitive, some research-based—to indicate that homes, and especially parents, contribute significantly to all aspects of children's development, including their success at school. The reasons relate to the central role of the home in children's lives, the importance of early development, and the cumulative nature of development.

The Central Role of the Home

Repeatedly, one finds statements asserting that parents, not teachers, are the primary agents of their children's development (for example, Silvern, 1988; van Leer Foundation, 1986). Various reasons can be cited for this conclusion. One is the sheer amount of time that children spend outside school. If up to the age of eighteen, children spend about 13 percent of their waking life at school, that means that parents, at least nominally, control 87 percent of students' waking time during their formative years (Walberg, 1984). These figures point to the importance of educational experiences in the home, in the community (since many children also spend significant amounts of time under the supervision of individuals who are not their parents), and in peer groups to promote the acquisition of knowledge and to foster the capacity to profit from further experience. Family experiences would seem to be particularly important since it is the home that provides the most permanent environment and point of reference for children (Landers and Myers, 1988).

More important perhaps than quantity of time are the circumstances provided for development. It is obvious that much development has taken place by the time children go to school. Most children will have established routine habits related to eating, sleeping, and washing. They will have acquired the gross motor skills involved in walking and running as well as the finer motor skills needed for such activities as drawing, building with blocks, and buttoning their coats. Socially, they will have developed to the extent that they can play with and share with others; emotionally, they will be able to cope with fear, anger, and frustration. They will also have learned to speak a language fluently and will have developed a wide range of perceptual and intellectual knowledge and skills (see Sears and Dowley, 1963). Such developments do not take place in the absence of certain basic conditions: a caring emotional environment, nutritional and health care, attention from adults, psychological stimulation, and a network of interpersonal relationships that are characterized by intensity, intimacy, and continuity over time.

Not least important in the home is nutritional and health care. In practice, it is often difficult to isolate the impact of such care on children's development since undernutrition is likely to occur in conditions of poverty, social disadvantage, and environmental deprivation, all of which may affect development. However, several deficiencies have been identified as having severe and long-lasting consequences for a child's development. These include iodine deficiency during pregnancy, zinc deficiency, and iron deficiency, the last of which is the most common nutritional disorder in the world. At a more general level, the available evidence strongly suggests that other forms of malnutrition during the early periods of a child's life can also have long-term adverse effects on cognitive development (Lozoff, 1989; Pollitt, 1990).

Malnutrition is a major problem throughout the world. World Health Organization statistics indicate that 40 to 60 percent of children suffer from mild to moderate undernutrition and 3 to 7 percent suffer from severe malnutrition. Although most prevalent in developing countries, problems of malnutrition are not uncommon in the industrialized world. Unfortunately, efforts to treat undernutrition do not appear to reverse all negative effects. Prevention is likely to be much more effective than therapeutic intervention at a later stage (Lozoff, 1989).

The contribution of the family to children's formal education is not restricted to providing an appropriate environment for physical development. Characteristics of the family and the relationships established by its members are also decisive factors influencing the development of children's ability to learn at school. A great many research studies in different countries provide evidence of an empirical relationship between a variety of indices of the home and a variety of measures of children's school-related behavior. One of the most widely quoted conclusions in educational research comes from the Equality of Educational Opportunity Survey, which contrasted the roles of school and home in school achievement: "Schools bring little influence to bear on a child's achievement that is independent of his background and general social context; . . . this very lack of an independent effect means that the inequalities imposed on children by their home, neighborhood and peer environment are carried along to become the inequalities with which they confront adult life at the end of school. For equality of educational opportunity must imply a strong effect of schools that is independent of the child's immediate social environment, and that strong independent effect is not present in American schools" (Coleman and others, 1966, p. 325). Although the conclusions of this study do not differ essentially from those of many other studies, they received considerably more attention, perhaps because the study had been sponsored by the U.S. government. We shall consider the evidence on relationships between home factors and school learning in detail in Chapters Three and Four.

The Importance of Early Development

Some of the research on relationships between environmental conditions and development has been interpreted to mean that early experiences may be crucial for later development. The findings of studies of the effects of deprivation at both human and animal levels in the development of the perceptual and cognitive skills of the young have been used to support this view. Some of these studies involved depriving animals of sensory experiences when young and examining the effects of this on the animal's later perceptual skills, intelligence, and problem-solving ability. In general, the findings indicated that the performance of animals deprived of certain types of experience early in life was seriously impaired at a later date. On the basis of such studies, Hebb (1949) argued that a great deal of perceptual learning is necessary before children see the world as the normal adult sees it. For example, he disputed the view that the human infant immediately perceives a square shape as a unified consistent structure, or whole. By its second year, the child may do so, but this is the result of a vast number of visual experiences and muscular explorations.

The popularization of this work in the writings of Bruner

(1961) and Hunt (1961) provided the basis for a reevaluation of the role of environmental factors in early child development. Interpreting the work, Bruner (1961) concluded that an environment that is impoverished—that is, one that is monotonous, with limited opportunities for different kinds of stimulation, discrimination, and manipulation—"provides an adult organism with reduced abilities to discriminate, with stunted strategies for coping with roundabout solutions, with less taste for exploratory behavior, and with a notably reduced tendency to draw inferences that serve to cement the disparate events of its environment" (p. 199).

Around the same time, although it did not deal with the extreme kind of deprivation described in Hebb's work, research on the development of children was underlining the importance of early childhood for later scholastic development. Bloom's (1964) analyses of longitudinal data from many studies indicate that growth or change at some stages of development is much more rapid than at other stages. Furthermore, for some of the most significant human characteristics, the most rapid period of development was found to be during the early phases. For such diverse characteristics as height, general intelligence, aggressiveness (in males), and dependency (in females), the most rapid growth was found to occur during the first five years of life.

At the time Bloom (1964) wrote about children's early experience and learning, he noted that the importance of early environmental and experiential influences was not fully recognized and that there seemed to be a general assumption that change in behavior could take place at any age or stage of development. His findings contributed to the widespread appreciation of the important role of the early years in the child's development and future school learning.

The research findings might have remained of academic interest only and might have had little impact on educational practice if they had not been reported at a time when Americans were looking critically at their educational system and particularly at the role of schools in dealing with problems of poverty (Madaus, Airasian, and Kellaghan, 1980). Concern was being expressed at the poor achievement and early dropout of children from homes of low socioeconomic status and the possible loss of talent to the nation as a result. This concern seemed to fit well with another dominant theme of the 1960s and 1970s — that of equality of opportunity. Taken together, these concerns pointed to a need for a greater understanding of the role of the home in the early development of children's scholastic knowledge and skills.

It is perhaps ironic that experience with preschool programs such as Head Start, which were designed to prepare children from disadvantaged backgrounds for school, helped considerably to bring into focus the critical importance of the home in children's scholastic development. It was partly because of the initially disappointing results from such programs that efforts to involve home and community agencies in children's education received a fresh impetus. Today, many commentators would view any attempt at intervention with children from disadvantaged backgrounds that did not include a home component as unlikely to be very effective.

The Cumulative Nature of Development

The implications of findings regarding the importance for schooling of early learning opportunities become clearer when we realize that much development is cumulative in nature. That is, developments at one period build on developments during an earlier period and in turn influence the nature of later developments (Bloom, 1964; Erickson, 1950; Hebb, 1949). This interpretation is supported by findings of studies of the relationship between development at different stages in the life span of individuals. In Bloom's (1964) analyses, many characteristics showed considerable stability over time. For example, the correlation between intelligence measured at age five and at age seventeen was about +.80, and between intelligence measured at age eight and at age seventeen almost +.90.

At the point at which children enter school, they already exhibit large differences in characteristics related to school learning. The findings of longitudinal studies of scholastic achievement are similar to those of studies of other human characteristics (such as intelligence) mentioned above. Using measures of general scholastic achievement, reading, and teacher's marks, Bloom (1964) found similar patterns of development for these achievements as for other characteristics. The curve for the development of performance on measures of general scholastic achievement showed that development during the early years in school up to the age of nine was relatively rapid and that the rate of growth was slower from age nine to eighteen.

Even though the importance of early development receives considerable support from research studies, we should not conclude that later environmental conditions are not also important for the child's development. Characteristics developed during the first two to three years are not necessarily permanent, although they may persist if the context that produced them does not change (Kagan, 1979). Further, events subsequent to a "sensitive" period of development may modify or even nullify characteristics that have been established (Bornstein, 1989). Early gains can be lost if the quality of experience depreciates but, by the same token, early losses may be made up if the development-fostering quality of experience improves (Hunt, 1979).

Conclusion

Although the expansion of schooling has no doubt brought great benefits to innumerable children, there is continuing concern about the ability of the school on its own to bring all children to acceptable levels of achievement. In particular, when children are poorly prepared to learn when they start school, it would seem that the best efforts of the school will not succeed in helping them reach adequate levels of achievement. The inference would seem justified that in the absence of adequate familial and social supports, the school will not do its job very well. Conversely, we can expect the educational system to work if the required supports are provided for students outside school (Caplan, Choy, and Whitmore, 1992).

Since in normal circumstances, the family plays a crucial role in children's development — because of the importance of early learning, because learning is cumulative, because children spend so much time at home—it seems reasonable to suggest that when children are likely to experience difficulties in school, the provision of assistance to families could be useful. This should not be taken to imply that the context in which the home is located and the role of community agencies are not important considerations also in providing optimal conditions for children's scholastic development. Any effort to support children's development and learning should take into account the context in which it is being implemented, as well as parents' needs and wishes. However, in this book, our main focus is the role of parents in the learning activities of the home. We feel that this focus is justified if for no other reason than that the greatest long-term benefits to the child seem to "accrue from changes in home environments over time" (van Leer Foundation, 1986, p. 7).

There are two further reasons for paying special attention to the home conditions of learning. First, demographic changes (which we will consider in Chapter Five) have resulted in reduced availability of human resources in many homes. For example, the decline of the extended family and the growth of one-parent families mean that children may not have the access that children in the past had to a range of persons to guide and assist their development. Proponents of parent programs sometimes see such programs as a substitute for the assistance that was once available in the extended family (Powell, 1988). And second, in considering whether to put resources into involving parents or into other institutions to promote children's development, one is likely to find that other approaches—for example, ones that involve preschools or day-care centers— are likely to be more expensive. They usually require professional and material resources that are often beyond the economic capabilities of communities or countries (van Leer Foundation, 1986).

In Chapters Three and Four, we examine research that sets out to identify the dimensions of home environments that correlate with school achievement. On the basis of this examination, in Chapter Nine we present the outline of a parent education

program that can form a useful focus for parent involvement.
The program has already been found, in one context at any
rate, to be effective in improving children's school achievement
(Janhom, 1983). Its main purpose is to help parents provide
their children with knowledge, skills, and attitudes that will allow
them to bridge the gap between home and school experiences.
We believe that many parents would welcome assistance in designing and implementing activities that research has indicated
would help their children in this task.

Improving the Home-School Partnership ■ TWO

In this chapter, we consider why schools and homes may appear divided in their efforts to achieve the shared objective of fostering children's development. We consider how problems can arise between the two institutions, particularly in terms of discontinuities in the experiences they provide for children. We then outline the particular problems of children who because of their poor scholastic performance have been described as "disadvantaged," "at risk," or "marginalized" in the educational system. Finally, we shall describe in general terms how educational systems have responded to the need to increase the involvement of families in schooling, by getting schools and homes to work together to support children's education.

Discontinuities Between Home and School

Although homes and schools ideally should play complementary and mutually reinforcing roles in children's education, major differences that exist between the two institutions, in their goals and in the circumstances in which they pursue those goals, may give rise to difficulties for some children.

The role of the home is perhaps most obvious in providing the conditions conducive to the early development of the child. Parents normally accept as basic obligations that they take care of their children's physical needs for food, clothing, nutrition,

17

and health. They also provide aspects of development that are closely related to the work of the school and to children's school learning, such as the development of language, self-concepts, interpersonal skills, values, and motivation to engage in the formal learning tasks of the school. Further, as children proceed through school, the home will be expected to support the school's activities by indicating to children that it values education and by providing the resources that children need to study.

For a variety of reasons, homes vary in the extent to which they foster knowledge, skills, and dispositions that support school learning. When the characteristics developed at home do not support school learning, it seems reasonable to conclude that the resultant discontinuity experienced by the children when they go to school will affect their scholastic performance. In the past, discontinuity between children's experiences at home and at school has been used to explain the poor school performance of immigrants in the United States and of children in colonial countries in Africa (Ogbu, 1982). During the 1920s, this view served as an important antidote to the belief that races could be ranked genetically in terms of their performance on newly developed intelligence tests.

Partly because research had not been carried out to support the discontinuity interpretation of school failure and partly because of the considerable amount of psychological research in the 1950s and 1960s on the effects of deprivation on human (and animal) development (which we summarized in Chapter One), an alternative view of the causes of school failure had become popular by the 1960s, when many intervention projects were planned to deal with the problem. According to that view, children's poor school performance was primarily the result of having been deprived of stimulating learning environments in their homes.

More recently, many educators, embarrassed by the implications of deficiencies in homes contained in this view, returned to the cultural discontinuity explanation of school failure. Again, the view gained popularity that children from certain backgrounds (for example, ethnic minority or poverty backgrounds) perform poorly at school, not because their backgrounds are deprived in any way — culturally or in terms of stimulating learning conditions — but because they had not the opportunity to acquire the content and style of learning that underlie the activities of schools (see Obgu, 1982, 1987; Philips, 1976).

Ogbu (1982, 1987, 1991) helped to clarify the cultural discontinuity hypothesis in his distinctions between the different types of discontinuity that may be associated with schooling. He pointed out that while some discontinuities are universal and are experienced by all children when they enter school, other discontinuities are experienced by only some groups of children. We will briefly outline the different types of discontinuities and look at some of the implications for helping children bridge the gap between home and school.

Discontinuities Experienced by All Children

Children have little knowledge of what to expect when they enter school (Dreeben, 1968). For many, their first day can be intimidating. Not only do children move from one physical environment to another, but many of the characteristics of the new environment are obviously very different from those at home (Bobbit and Paolucci, 1986; Comer, 1984; Griffore and Bubolz, 1986; Ogbu, 1982, 1987; Silvern, 1988; Wood, 1988).

Perhaps the first thing that children notice at school is that they are moving from life in a small group of people to life in a crowd. As Jackson (1968) has pointed out: "Learning to live in a classroom involves, among other things, learning to live in a crowd. . . . Most of the things that are done in school are done with others, or at least in the presence of others, and this fact has profound implications for determining the quality of a student's life" (p. 10).

Another difference is the way in which space and time are organized. While the home is marked by informality and freedom in the use of time and space, in school the children are allocated to classrooms and seats and work to a predicable daily schedule. Normally, they may not move from one school area to another without teacher direction, and they are limited in when they may talk to others and in what they may talk about.

All children will also find that they have to adjust to inter-personal relationships in school that differ markedly from those in the home in their intensity, form, and function (Kontos, 1992). While homes are generally marked by intimate, continuous, and particularistic relationships, the relationships at school are less familiar, more transitory, and universalistic. Teachers do not get too close to students and are expected to treat all in much the same way. Furthermore, teachers exercise considerable authority over students, to a large extent controlling their lives within the confines of the school—what classroom they are in, when they work and when they play, and what they learn. This degree of authority will be a new experience for many children.

Concern in the school with literacy rather than with oracy will also be new for many children. Very soon after coming to school, children begin to learn to read and to communicate in writing. Some, of course, will have commenced these activities at home and so will experience less discontinuity. However, for all children—even those who have experienced reading and writing before coming to school—the shift in emphasis will be noticeable.

At a more general level, children come to realize that the main focus of learning in the school is on cognitive performance. Further, the types and conditions of learning are likely to differ markedly from most of the types and conditions of learning that the children had previously experienced. In the home, children learn in a natural and realistic context as the need arises to do such things as tie their shoelaces, cook food, or operate media equipment. By contrast, learning in school is formal, deliberate, and conscious, taking place day in and day out, whether or not it seems to have any particular purpose. This means that much school learning may have no immediate context or use. Indeed, much of school learning is purposely decontextualized, being directed toward the development of the use of symbols, concepts, and information-processing skills. The learning of mathematics provides an obvious example. Although children may learn basic mathematical concepts through the use of concrete materials (for example, using blocks to add and subtract), ultimately mathematics is concerned with symbols that may have no direct referent in the real world. Further evidence of the decontextualization of learning can be found in the way schools teach skills that can be used in a variety of contexts. Thus, students are taught reading so that they will be able to access further knowledge; writing so that they can communicate knowledge; and various techniques for finding, processing, and organizing information.

These distinctions between home and school learning are perhaps too sharply drawn. We are all aware of schools that try to make learning informal and that attempt to provide experiences that foster students' self-concepts and values. We also know of homes where children learn to read before they go to school and that provide a variety of materials and experiences to support children during their formal educational careers. Indeed, it is a central contention of this book that many homes are, and many more can be, organized to promote intellectual development and learning, which in turn will help to ensure that school learning proceeds smoothly. This should not be taken to mean that homes should attempt to replicate the learning situation of the school or to teach school subjects. Rather, it means that homes should seek to exploit the educational potential of parent-child relationships and of daily family routines to develop in children the ability to find, process, and organize information, as well as to develop values and attitudes conducive to learning.

Discontinuities Experienced by Children in Non-Western Countries at Western-Type Schools

Although all children experience some discontinuity between home and school, children living in non-Western countries who attend Western-type schools must experience much greater discontinuity, since the overlap in environments between their homes and schools is less than the overlap between a Western home and school. Obgu (1982) draws on Gay and Cole's (1967) study of the Kpelle in Liberia to illustrate the kinds of problems that children in non-Western countries might face at school. He points out that learning in the Kpelle home is likely to be largely nonverbal and based on tradition, thus obviating the need to provide explanations. Further, in the specific area of mathematics, Kpelle children will be at a disadvantage at school because their language does not have words for *zero* or *number,* while terms such as *middle, half,* and *many* lack precise meaning. Indeed, the whole of the Western school's curriculum (reading, mathematics, science) would appear to be alien to the Kpelle child's traditional culture. As a consequence, the school tends to be isolated from the cultural system in which it is located, making it difficult for children to adapt to it and for homes to reinforce what is taught there. Despite these difficulties, the Kpelle and other non-Western peoples accept schooling because of the benefits they see it will provide, somehow managing to overcome discontinuities relating to cognitive skills, values, rules of interaction and communication, and learning strategies.

The case of the Kpelle can only be taken as illustrative of the kinds of discontinuity problems that may arise for a child from a non-Western culture who attends a Western school. Even within Africa, there are vast differences between ethnic groups in their physical environments, their diets, the nature of their traditional economies, and their cultural institutions, all of which could have implications for the kind of cognitive and personality characteristics fostered in a culture. The idea of regarding the problems of all children from non-Western cultures in Western schools as similar becomes even more questionable when we consider the vast range of cultures that are spread across the rest of the world. Because of this variation, our understanding of the problems experienced by children from non-Western backgrounds in Western schools remains extremely limited.

Discontinuities Experienced by Minority Group Children

Other groups of children who are likely to experience cultural discontinuities at school are minority and subordinate group children. Examples of such groups in the United States are blacks, American Indians, Chicanos, and Puerto Ricans. In other terminology, many members of these groups would be described as "marginalized," "disadvantaged," or "at risk" in the school situation, resulting in low academic achievement and high dropout rates.

A number of research studies point to characteristics of

the homes of minority groups that may create problems for children at school, placing them at a greater disadvantage than children from the mainstream culture. For example, differences between Hispanic and white families have been found in parental teaching behavior and in other educationally relevant aspects of the parent-child relationship. Parent-child interactions in the average white home have been found to resemble more closely the types of interaction that one would expect to find in a school than do parent-child interactions in the average Hispanic family. As a result, the Hispanic child is more likely to experience discontinuity between the teaching practices and styles of home and school. Such discontinuity, which will be particularly abrupt for children whose parents had relatively little schooling, has been advanced as an explanation of the low levels of school achievement and the high dropout rate that are found among Hispanics and other minority group children (Laosa, 1982).

Children from minority groups may experience difficulties beyond ones associated with parental teaching style. For example, Ogbu (1987) has identified difficulties that he attributes to "the nature of the history, subordination, and exploitation of the minorities, *and* the nature of the minorities' own instrumental and expressive responses to their treatment, which enter into the process of their schooling" (p. 317). Thus, for Ogbu, the responses of minority group children to home-school discontinuities may be compounded by their position in society and their perceptions of dismal postschool opportunities. Having compared themselves to the dominant group, they conclude that their position is subordinate and that they have been subject to exploitation. The result is that, even though they may know a good deal about the culture of the dominant group, they do not accept it for themselves because of its negative associations in their history and experience.

Discontinuities Experienced by
Immigrant Children in Western Countries

At first glance, immigrant children might appear to be at the greatest disadvantage of all on entering school. Certainly, in terms of a cultural discontinuity hypothesis, their position would not seem to be any better than that of indigenous minority group children. Both sets of children are likely to have experiences that differ from school practice in communication strategies, in rules of interaction, and in the degree of literacy in their home backgrounds. However, immigrant families are faced with the additional problem of trying to establish themselves in an alien society, so the discontinuities faced by their children at school in language and culture would often appear to be very great. Despite these handicaps, some immigrant groups in the United States, particularly ones from Asia, perform very well at school, certainly better than indigenous minority group children (see, for example, Coleman and others, 1966).

There is no obvious explanation for this phenomenon. It may be that immigrant groups differ from indigenous minority groups in their response to the cultural and language problems facing them, perceiving cultural differences as "barriers to be overcome," rather than as "markers of identity to be maintained" (Ogbu, 1987, p. 327). Even if language and communication problems are common to both groups, Ogbu points out that the groups differ in their approach to and success in school because of differences between the groups in their experiences of postschool opportunities. Unlike indigenous groups, immigrants may see their present condition as temporary, to be improved, in the case of their children at any rate, by education. Further, immigrants may take the situation they left in their homeland as a point of reference rather than the local dominant groups, with which indigenous groups compare themselves. Compared to the situation they left behind, their present situation may seem preferable.

Ogbu's (1982) description of the educational performances of Buraku children in Japan and in the United States can be taken as illustrating these points: "In Japan, Buraku children continue massively to under perform in school when compared with children of the dominant Ippan group. One of the explanations for their low performance in Japan has to do with language, communication, and interaction differences. But in the United States, . . . the Buraku do at least as well at school as their other Japanese and American counterparts" (p. 303).

The contrast between the performance of the Buraku at home and abroad suggests that when people emigrate to escape from an oppressive social structure and to gain access to greater opportunity, particularly for their children, their attitudes to and performance in education may alter radically. While this may be so for some groups, we are left with the puzzle as to why some immigrant groups perform much better than others in the educational system.

Implications of Discontinuities Between Home and School

The discontinuity hypothesis is based on the premise that an environment fosters the development of the particular knowledge, skills, learning styles, and values that have adaptive value for individuals living in it. Since environments differ, the competencies they nourish will also differ. A consequence of this is that when people move from one setting to another, we would expect their success in meeting the demands of the new environment to depend on the extent to which they can apply the competencies developed in the original environment. When we apply this reasoning to children making the transition from home to school, we conclude that since homes and schools differ in the demands they make on individuals, all children will experience some problems with discontinuity when they go to school. Further, since homes also differ among themselves in the competencies they foster, some children will be more disadvantaged than others in making the transition.

Children's problems with discontinuity can be eased in at least two ways. First, the overlap in home and school experiences can be increased so as to reduce the extent of the discontinuity. This can be done in the home by providing the child with school-related experiences and in the school by taking account of and adapting teaching to the competencies the child has acquired at home. If the advantage that middle-class children have at school can be interpreted in terms of the discontinuity hypothesis as arising from the great amount of experiences that their homes share with schools, then programs that familiarize children with the tasks of the school should help smooth the transition from home to school of children whose experiences at home are not closely related to those at school.

A second strategy is to demonstrate to children how knowledge and skills acquired at home can be applied in the context of school. However, the empirical evidence relating to people's ability to transfer learning acquired in one context to another is complex. On the one hand, there is evidence that an automatic transfer of skills learned in specific contexts and in relation to particular units of knowledge cannot be assumed. This point can be illustrated with the findings of several studies that indicate that if children have been reared in a non-Western (for example, African) environment, they are likely to experience difficulty when faced with the task of abstracting from the immediately perceptible aspects of unfamiliar objects. For example, Yoruba children in Nigeria have been found to have difficulty sorting unfamiliar colored geometric shapes on the basis of form but to have no difficulty sorting objects with which they were familiar (Kellaghan, 1968). Similarly, Mano children in Liberia, for whom dealing with rice is an important economic activity, have been found to readily sort rice into different categories. American students, on the other hand, when faced with this task, exhibited the kinds of problems and hesitancy that African children showed with the colored geometric shapes (Irwin, Schafer, and Feiden, 1974).

While the findings of these studies point to difficulties in applying skills learned in one situation to the solution of problems in a different context, at the same time, some aspects of cognitive skill are obviously quite general. Although it is clear that effective performance in a particular domain requires specific knowledge (you can't play chess without knowing the rules), there is also evidence that general cognitive skills can be developed that have wide application for problem solving, inventive thinking, learning, and decision making (Perkins and Solomon, 1989). Individuals can be helped to apply skills in new contexts if similarities between contexts and tasks are identified for them. Language is a major resource for this activity since it can be used to encode relevant relationships and to point out important connections between contexts and tasks that students may not identify without assistance (Laboratory of Comparative Human Cognition, 1983). When connections are verbalized and made explicit, the child is helped to see the relationships between tasks in different contexts and to appreciate how skills already developed in one context (the home) can be applied in another (the school).

Although our focus in this book is on how homes can help children deal with discontinuities between home and school, this should not be taken to imply that schools do not have an important role to play also. If school personnel are familiar with children's home backgrounds, they too can help children integrate their home and school experiences by taking account in their teaching of the categories of meaning that children bring with them to school. And just like parents, teachers can also use language to make explicit to children the similarities that may underlie dissimilarities in their experience, thus enabling children to apply in the context of the school the knowledge and skills they have acquired in their homes.

The Problem of Disadvantage

In considering discontinuities experienced by minority group children, we noted that the terms *marginalized, educationally disadvantaged,* and *at risk* are sometimes used to describe the conditions under which such children live. The terms have been defined in various ways, but most definitions imply a discontinuity between chidren's home and community experiences and the demands of schooling. For example, at a UNESCO meeting in Hamburg in 1967, a definition was reached that regarded students as being disadvantaged if, because of sociocultural reasons, they entered the school system with knowledge, skills, and attitudes that made adjustment difficult and impeded learning (Passow, 1970).

Lest we assume that disadvantage always originates in the home, Pallas, Natriello, and McDill (1989) remind us that students may also be disadvantaged if they have been exposed to inappropriate educational experiences in the community or the school. The key indicators of educational disadvantage that they list, however, all relate to the home or community: minority racial/ethnic group identity, living in a poverty household, living in a single-parent family, having a poorly educated mother, and having a home language that differs from that used in school. These indicators are not independent of each other. For example, status in a racial or ethnic minority group is often associated with poverty; so also is living in a single-parent family. This means that some children may be classified as disadvantaged on the basis of two or more indicators.

The problem of disadvantage manifests itself in school in poor educational performance. The signs of difficulty are usually in evidence from a very early stage. On entering schools, children from disadvantaged backgrounds are more poorly equipped with the knowledge and skills required for success than are children from more advantaged backgrounds. Furthermore, although the evidence on this point is not entirely consistent (Martin, 1979), the achievement gap between children from advantaged and disadvantaged backgrounds tends to widen as children progress through school. For example, Coleman and others (1966) found that for students in the nonmetropolitan southern and southwestern regions of the United States, the average difference between black and white students in reading comprehension increased between grades 6 and 12. In a study in England and Wales, approximately 1 standard deviation separated high- from low-socioeconomic-background children on achievement tests at age eight; by age eleven, the average scores for the groups differed even more (Douglas, 1964).

Indicators are useful for pointing to fairly readily identifiable characteristics of families (or students) that are frequently associated with disadvantage. However, the presence of an indicator does not necessarily mean that a family or student is disadvantaged. Much less does it mean that it is the cause of disadvantage. Take racial/ethnicity identity, for example. Even though black students in Britain leave school at an earlier age than white students and perform less well on examinations at the age of sixteen, recent results from classroom tests (Standard Attainment Tasks) found that among seven-year-olds, 10 percent of blacks compared to 6 percent of whites gained the top grade in mathematics and 19 percent of blacks compared to 18 percent of whites gained the top grade in science (Hymas, 1992). Among the students who did particularly well, scoring top marks in English, mathematics, and science, was Natalie, who lives in central Birmingham. Natalie's mother, whose parents came to Britain from Jamaica in the mid-1950s, would like her daughter to go to a leading university. She describes some of the factors associated with Natalie's success: "We encourage her at home. She loves reading and she doesn't watch a lot of television. I stress to her the importance of doing well at school. I didn't do very well and left when I was 15. I really regret that now and I want my children to do well" (Hymas, 1992, p. 3). The principal teacher in the school also offered an explanation: "It all depends on having high expectations of the children and strong parental support. All ethnic groups want their children to do well, and it's our job to deliver a quality product to ensure they do" (Hymas, 1992, p. 3).

These comments underline the importance of two things in considering disadvantage. First, it is important to look beyond indicators or labels, such as ethnic identity or social class, when searching for reasons why some students perform poorly at school. And second, home factors (as well as school factors) play a role in school success and failure. As we proceed through this book, we hope to identify the characteristics of homes that foster school learning.

Schools and Homes Working Together

If homes are important for learning, what steps, we may ask, have been taken to get parents involved in their children's formal education? The United States has a long tradition of such involvement. Most school districts have a local parent-teacher association or parent-teacher-student organization to ensure that parents know about and can influence educational issues. At the national level, the National Congress for Parents and Teachers has been active in lobbying for such things as school safety standards, health programs, and television programming for children.

In European countries, the situation is more complex. Conditions vary because of differences between countries in traditions of home-school cooperation, in legal arrangements, and in ideology. Some countries, in fact, once had policies that set out specifically to limit the influence of the home on children. For example, efforts to promote the socialist way of life in the Soviet Union in the 1920s involved attempts to limit the influence of family values on children's development. (The policy was reversed in the 1940s). In Sweden, a belief that strategies for school-based compensatory education would contribute to the reduction of social stratification also led to attempts to diminish the influence of the home (Schleicher, 1989).

Nowadays, in at least one European country (Germany), parents have a right to take part in educational policy decisions at school and regional levels. In other countries, parents are involved in curriculum decision making (Denmark, Norway). In the Netherlands, public schools (which are supported by local communities) and private schools (mainly church-related) have a tradition of strong parent committees at school and community levels. By contrast, parents in France appear to have had little success in challenging the power of the central bureaucracy and the teaching profession; their involvement in schools is restricted to concern with peripheral areas, such as extracurricular activities and school transport (Schleicher, 1989).

Since the 1960s, several countries have developed programs to promote parent involvement in education that go well beyond traditional parent-teacher associations in the activities they propose for parents. For the most part, these programs focus on families in "disadvantaged" areas where children are considered to be "at risk" of failure in the educational system, and they attempt to involve parents intimately in their children's education. Today in the United States, the new parent involvement programs are seen as representing a substantial public commitment to the provision of educational opportunity to disenfranchised populations (Powell, 1988).

Relevant legal developments in the United States that emphasize the importance of parent involvement include Chapter 1 legislation and the Hawkins-Stafford School Improvement

Amendments of 1988 (D'Angelo and Adler, 1991). Partly as a result of these initiatives, a great variety of approaches to getting families to work with schools as knowledgeable partners can be found across the country at national, state, district, and school levels (see Epstein, 1991b). George Bush's National Education Strategy to move the nation toward the education goals adopted by the president and state governors for the year 2000 acknowledges that "parents are the keys to their children's education, and there is no part of the America 2000 strategy in which they do not have an important role" (*America 2000. An Education Strategy,* 1991, p. 44). Particular attention is drawn to the role of parents in achieving the first goal, which is that "all children in America will start school ready to learn" (p. 19).

In Australia, an awareness of the considerable influence that parents can exercise upon children's learning of specific subjects at school has led to the development of parental involvement in school curricula. Several experimental programs aimed at helping parents support their children's learning of mathematics, one of the areas about which most parents felt uncertain, have been set up on the assumption that the success of new mathematics curricula will largely depend on the active support of families and the wider community (Stephens and Carss, 1986).

A trend is also apparent in European countries to augment the role of the family in education. New organizational frameworks, such as school management boards and national parent councils, have been developed to promote cooperation between home and school. Means are also being explored to cope with specific social, educational, and attitudinal obstacles to cooperation (Schleicher, 1989). Programs that focus on families in disadvantaged areas are now in operation in several countries. In Ireland, for example, teachers have been appointed in disadvantaged areas to liaise between schools, homes, and communities with the aims of maximizing active participation of students in the learning process, promoting active cooperation between schools and other statutory and voluntary agencies that provide services for students and their families, and raising awareness in parents of their own capacities to enhance their children's educational progress and to assist them in developing relevant skills (Ryan, 1992).

Parent involvement programs exhibit a variety of dimensions, exemplified by the many types of strategies that have been developed to promote such involvement (see Chrispeels, 1991; Davies, 1991; Epstein, 1987b; Fine, 1989; Solomon, 1991; Swap, 1990). One way to categorize these strategies is by the extent to which they focus on formal learning and teaching. Activities that focus on teaching and learning may be described as *proximal;* those that do not relate directly to teaching and learning but to supporting these activities may be described as *intermediate;* more remote educational activities may be regarded as *distal.* There are many examples of strategies that can be characterized in these ways.

Proximal

1. Parent involvement in learning activities at home, including those directed toward development of skills in problem solving, critical thinking, or conversation; provision of facilities that help school learning; supervision of homework; work with children on mathematics, language arts, music, art, and so on.
2. Parent involvement in instruction at school (for example, as teacher aide).

Intermediate

1. Communication between schools and parents regarding school programs and children's school progress (for example, notes, meetings).
2. Assistance in school with noninstructional activities, such as field trips, library work, and playground supervision.
3. Attendance at workshops, lectures, and discussions on school policies or on home conditions that promote learning.
4. Relationships with teachers through structures in schools that provide support for and coordinate activities that promote and sustain the parental role in education.

Distal

1. Basic provision for health, nutrition, safety, and general well-being of children.
2. Parental involvement in governance and advocacy on behalf of the school (for example, in a parent-teacher association or on a school management board).
3. Attendance at general education programs for parents (for example, self-development, cookery, language, literacy).
4. Contact with community resources, which may or may not be formally organized, that provide support services for families and children.

Programs designed to improve the involvement of families living in disadvantaged areas have focused on one or more of these dimensions. As we shall see in Chapter Six, many programs adopt a comprehensive approach, providing a wide range of services for children and their families. Others are more focused, choosing to involve parents in extending the range of their verbal interactions with their children or in helping their children learn reading or mathematics.

Conclusion

In this chapter, we considered discontinuities between home and school for the most part in terms of children's group membership — living in a non-Western culture or in a minority indigenous or immigrant group in a Western country. We have reason to believe that the environments associated with these group memberships teach different capabilities and that these capabilities have greater adaptation value in some environments than in others (R. W. Henderson, 1981). We also have reason to believe that differences between the competencies fostered in homes and schools may create problems for children in adapting to the work of the school.

However, the cultural discontinuity hypothesis cannot account for all the variance in school achievement that is found even at a very early age among children. For one thing, it is clear that some minority groups are much more successful in school than others, despite the fact that they would appear to face huge discontinuities between their home culture and the culture of the school. Further, we know that within any group, children vary in the degree to which they are prepared for the work of school and in the extent to which they are successful at school. Among all groups — culturally dominant, immigrant, or minority — some members do succeed at school. Indeed, it is a major problem of the cultural discontinuity hypothesis, as it is of hypotheses of school failure based on social-class membership, that it does not deal adequately with the variance in school achievement that one finds between one home and another.

Another way of looking at school failure is to regard culture (or race or socioeconomic status) as not being the only determinant of the basic elements of homes that promote creative development and facilitate school success (Good, 1986). Rather, since homes in all circumstances play a major role in children's development, it is worth attempting to identify the features of homes that seem to contribute most to children's scholastic development. If we could specify those features, it might then be possible to construct a program that would provide school-relevant experiences for children in homes in which those features are not well developed. While it would be overoptimistic to expect that such a program would be successful in all situations, at the same time, in the light of evidence we shall consider later in this book, it does not seem unrealistic to suggest that many families can increase the amount of support they provide for their children's education, whatever their ethnic or cultural background. As we shall see in Chapter Eight, programs in a variety of situations in which discontinuities would be expected to exist between home and school have not been without success in helping parents (especially mothers) improve the scholastic performance of their children. By conveying to parents, and through them to their children, a corpus of know-how and values, both parents and children can be assisted to cope with the demands of the formal educational system. If, in time, that can help young people from whatever background to acquire the skills and knowledge that they will need for employment and for participation in the social and cultural life of society, it will surely have been worth the effort.

As we have seen, many examples of efforts to improve the home-school interface can be found throughout the world. These vary considerably in the extent to which they focus on providing support for the learning activities of children. Ones that concern themselves with activities that impinge only remotely on children's learning (for example, programs in cookery for parents) are less likely to impact children's school learning than activities that more directly involve parents in, for example, the development in their children of skills in problem solving, critical thinking, or conversation. However, even programs that are not closely related to children's learning can be useful as a first step in increasing parents' interest and involvement in the work of the school. Ultimately, one would hope that all parents would grow in appreciation of the vital role they can play in their children's learning and act accordingly.

THREE ◼ Family Characteristics and School Learning

This is the first of two chapters in which research findings on the relationships between school learning and home background are considered. The studies reviewed in this chapter used socioeconomic status (SES), social class, and family configuration to characterize home background—that is, family status and structure. Some went beyond these variables and examined associated parental characteristics (attitudes, interests). In Chapter Four, we will consider research that set out to identify activities in homes that are associated with school learning; we will find that the association between learning and home activities is much closer than the association examined in this chapter, between learning and family status and structure.

Various indices of school learning have been used in the studies described here and in the next chapter. Many studies used measures of children's achievement (for example, in language, mathematics, science), while others also used measures of ability (for example, general scholastic ability, verbal ability, spatial ability). The measures most frequently used were standardized norm-referenced tests, though some studies used grade-point averages, student examination results, or teacher ratings.

As well as measuring scholastic achievements and abilities—or instead of doing so—some studies examined relationships between home background and the highest level in the educational system reached by students—the highest grade completed at high school, college education, or professional or graduate study. This is sometimes called school attainment and essentially is equivalent to the number of years of schooling that a student completes. We would, of course, expect educational achievements to be positively correlated with educational attainment. That is, the longer that students stay at school and the higher the grade level they complete, the greater should be their range of knowledge, skills, and competencies.

The Role of Socioeconomic Status

Although the concept of socioeconomic status and an associated concept, social class, appear frequently in research as indices of home background, there is lack of agreement on precisely what the terms mean or how to measure them. In one interpretation, social class is taken to represent a style or way of life. In another, it represents power over resources and people. In yet another, social class indicates the esteem or status of a family in society.

Among the indices that have been used to assign a family to a socioeconomic status or social class are parental occupation, level of parental education, parental income, and the prestige of the breadwinner's occupation. Families are often categorized as being either middle-class or lower-class, but usually a finer discrimination is employed to provide a greater number of categories in which the middle-class category is divided into professional, clerical, and white-collar occupations and the lower-class category is divided into skilled, semiskilled, and unskilled occupations. The various indices measuring socioeconomic status have been found to be highly intercorrelated (Kahl and Davis, 1955).

Studies of the relationship between socioeconomic status and scholastic behavior go back to the beginning of this century. Reviews of such studies indicate that the level of socioeconomic status or of social class accounts for an average of under 10 percent of variance in a variety of measures of scholastic ability and achievement in studies that used income as the index of family circumstances and an average of about 4 percent of variance in studies that used occupation as the family index (see Kahl and Davis, 1955; Lavin, 1965; White, 1982).

What is it about socioeconomic status that might affect children's scholastic ability and achievements? In attempting to answer this question, a number of investigations have focused on aspects of family functioning and, in particular, on the behavior of mothers with their children. For example, Hess and Shipman (1965, 1967) observed differences between mothers of different social classes in the way they instructed their children in three simple learning tasks. One task involved sorting plastic toys (cars, spoons, chairs) by color and function; in another task, eight blocks of differing color, size, and shape had to be sorted by two characteristics (for example, color, size) simultaneously; the third task involved copying designs. Each mother was first taught the task and then asked to teach her child. Some of the mothers came from homes in which the breadwinner held a professional or managerial occupation; others came from homes in which the breadwinner held a skilled, semiskilled, or unskilled occupation. A number of differences were found between mothers from the two types of background in the strategies they used to teach their children. For example, mothers from professional homes were better than mothers from manual occupation homes at verbally instructing their children to help them understand the tasks. They were also better at structuring the task, saying, "I'm going to show you how," and at providing positive reinforcement for children who made correct responses, saying, "That's right." Furthermore, the maternal teaching variables were found to be related to the children's level of success on the tasks as well as to measures of the children's verbal ability.

The authors interpret the differences in maternal behavior in terms of class-related availability of options in society. For example, families in which the breadwinner works in a manual occupation are perceived to have relatively few options from which to choose in the major areas of their life. They are often remote from sources of power in society and may be subject to informal controls and economic exploitation. "In this position of weakness in the social structure, parents are little inclined to encourage their children to consider alternatives, to develop criteria for choice, and to learn the basic elements of decision-making and anticipating future consequences of present actions" (Hess and Shipman, 1967, p. 59). If this interpretation is correct, then social-class membership, in particular the power associated with different positions in the social-class hierarchy, can affect the behavior of the members.

Other investigators have gone on to study the extent to which the conditions of life experienced by members of different social classes affect their ideas of social reality, their value systems, and their perceptions of their children and of the role of education. In addressing these questions, differences between social classes in aspects of their value systems have been documented. For example, the values of manual workers tend to center on conformity to external prescriptions, while those of professional parents tend to center on self-direction (see Duvall, 1946; Kohn, 1963). Like Hess and Shipman, Kohn attributes these differences in values to differences in the conditions of life between lower and higher socioeconomic groups. However, he focuses particularly on how occupational demands might contribute to this situation, pointing out that higher-class occupations require a greater degree of self-direction than lower-class occupations, which require individuals in larger measure to follow explicit rules that have been set down by somebody in authority. It is these differences in occupational circumstances, as well as other aspects of the social-class hierarchy, that are reflected in the value that is assigned to conformity in the case of lower socioeconomic families and the value that is assigned to the development of autonomy and self-direction in the case of higher socioeconomic families. These values, in turn, are reflected in child-rearing practices.

Other sources to which we might look in attempting to explain class-related differences in behavior generally, and in scholastic behavior in particular, are the belief systems associated with class—that is, statements about how the world operates that often serve to justify values and norms (Peterson, 1979). In reflecting on the teaching strategies of parents, McGillicuddy-DeLisi (1982) concluded that "beliefs were mediating variables between family constellation, SES, and parental practices. That is, one source of parents' behaviors with their children is the parents' beliefs about children in general, and it is the belief system of parents that is affected by background factors such as SES and number or spacing of children" (p. 297). Some commentators see social class as reflecting much more than belief systems. They regard it as a gross index of life-style; that is, of shared values or tastes as reflected primarily in consumption patterns and in the evaluation of intangible and/or public goods (Zablocki and Kanter, 1976). In addition to beliefs and values, social class may also subsume a variety of other variables, such as attitudes, patterns of parent-child interaction, and motivations (R. W. Henderson, 1981; Marjoribanks, 1979a).

One aspect of social class that has received considerable attention in exploring the relationship between socioeconomic background and scholastic development is language. Bernstein (1971, 1973, 1975), who inspired much research in this area, took the view that language reflects the experiences of members of different classes at work, in the community, and at home. He observed that individuals in lower socioeconomic groups live in tightly knit communities and have to fit into prescribed roles at work and at home, roles that tend to be traditional and to minimize individuality; people in higher socioeconomic groups are less integrated into a community structure, have greater freedom and autonomy in work, and have greater discretion in role performance in the family. These differences, he claims, are translated into different uses of language.

In the case of lower socioeconomic groups, Bernstein believes the translation results in what he calls a "restricted" language code, in which language is embedded in context, reflects the status of individuals, and minimizes the need to make one's meaning explicit. The conditions of higher socioeconomic groups, on the other hand, lead to use of what he calls an "elaborated" language code. Because the behavior of members of higher socioeconomic groups is less context-based and more individualistic, principles and operations have to be made more explicit in language so that the meaning of individual actions can be explored and explained.

An example of how the use of language in different socio-economic groups may have implications for children's learning is provided by Bernstein in two vignettes of a mother and child riding a bus. In the pair from the lower socioeconomic group, the mother's mode of control relies on commands with little explanation (for example, "Hold on tight") and reflects a hierarchical view of the adult-child relationship ("I told you to hold on tight, didn't I?"). In the pair from the middle socioeconomic group, on the other hand, the relationship is less hierarchical, and the mother provides a learning opportunity by using language to explore the situation in which she and her child find themselves. ("If you don't hold on tight, you will be thrown forward and you will fall." "If the bus stops suddenly, you'll jerk forward on to the seat in front.")

An important educational consequence of these two different approaches to language is that the relatively context-independent "universalistic" system, which is used in the middle-class home, is the one that is used in the schools. Although in theory the system is open to all, in practice children in the lower-status home may not have acquired it, placing them at a disadvantage in school relative to children from middle-class homes.

Bernstein's view is so wide ranging—connecting aspects of community, work, and family life to language and ultimately to education—that it is not surprising that aspects of it have been challenged. For example, while studies of the use of language by black children in the United States did reveal a form of language that differed from more standard forms, the language, especially when observed in informal situations, was found to reveal a coherent inner logic and complex structure. Further, complicated and abstract ideas could be expressed in it (Labov, 1972). These observations indicate that it would be wrong to conclude that different forms of language reflect inferior or superior modes of cognition or of thinking.

However, it does not seem unreasonable to assume that differences in systems of values, beliefs, language, and knowledge may be due, in part at least, as Bernstein and others have suggested, to differences in the basic conditions of life at different levels of the social order and that occupational, educational, and economic differences between the classes may all contribute to these differences. Further, it would not be unreasonable to expect that the values, beliefs, and linguistic codes developed in a social class often play a functional role in the context of the demands made on individual members of that class (Kohn, 1963). However, it may also be that some beliefs, values, and linguistic codes that are transmitted from generation to generation cease over time to serve a functional role and, in particular, may not be functional in dealing with situations such as schooling that fall outside the traditional culture.

Although attempts to explain differences between families and children's scholastic performance in terms of social class or socioeconomic status have given rise to many interesting and provocative hypotheses, their value for the educator is limited. If one accepted Bernstein's position, one might, for example, provide programs that would give greater access to children from low socioeconomic backgrounds to the use of "elaborated" language codes. However, the teacher will know that families within any one socioeconomic group vary considerably in a variety of ways (in their beliefs, values, attitudes, motivations, and parent-child interactions) as well as in the performance at school of their children. Faced with the problem of doing something here and now with a particular child, an explanation of the child's performance in terms of socioeconomic background is not likely to be very helpful. Indeed, recourse to such an explanation may be damaging if teachers use children's social-class membership to set their expectations for children, expecting poorer school performance from low-status children than from high-status children, and then proceeding to treat the children in accordance with those expectations (Brophy and Good, 1974).

The Role of Family Structure

Unlike studies of socioeconomic background, studies of family structure go beyond the use of status variables to examine relationships between aspects of families (family size, sibling sex and spacing, and birth position in family) and scholastic ability and achievement. The interaction between these family variables can be quite complex so that the influence on scholastic ability or achievement of any one of them (for example, birth position in family) may be modified by the configuration of other characteristics (for example, sex of child or spacing between siblings). However, a number of general conclusions emerge from the research in this area (Cicirelli, 1978).

First, a consistent finding is that there is a negative relationship between family size and measured abilities and achievements. For example, for an almost complete sample of eleven-year-old Scottish children, Thomson (1949) found that mean score on a test of verbal ability decreased as size of family increased. Many other investigators report basically similar findings (Belmont and Marolla, 1973; Burt, 1946; Douglas, 1964; Kellaghan and Macnamara, 1972; Marjoribanks, 1976; Nisbet and Entwistle, 1967; Tabah and Sutter, 1954). The amount of variance accounted for by family size in these studies ranges between 4 and 10 percent.

The effects of educational aspects of the home background on children have commonly been considered in attempting to explain this relationship. Several commentators have regarded amount of parent contact with the child as important (for example, Anastasi, 1956). If a child's intellectual ability depends on the amount of parental attention he or she receives, then it is obvious that a child in a small family should be better off since parents in this family will have more time to spend with the child than would parents in a larger family. In the smaller family, one would expect more opportunities for verbal interaction between parents and children; there may also be emotional benefits. There is some evidence, however, that this argument may not hold for families at all socioeconomic levels. Family size, which directly reflects the amount of attention available for children, is more likely to affect verbal ability and achievement in families in which the father has a low occupational level than in families in which the father has a high occupational level (Marjoribanks, 1974a; Marjoribanks, Walberg, and Bargen, 1975).

The second general finding that emerges from studies of the relationship between family structure and scholastic performance is that increased spacing between children's births reduces the decrement in scholastic performance that is normally associated with increase in family size (Rosenberg and Sutton-Smith, 1969; Tabah and Sutter, 1954). This finding supports the interpretation that the effect of family size on children's scholastic development is a function of the amount of time and attention that parents can give children.

Third, studies of the relationship between a child's birth position in the family and scholastic performance yield different conclusions. A child's birth position, of course, is related to family size. If you are the tenth child, you must be a member of a large family and so are subject to the disadvantages of being in such a family. Thus, family size may account in part for the finding in some studies that general-ability test scores of children decline with increasing birth order, with some exceptions (Belmont and Marolla, 1973), and that school failure rates or assignment to a special school are also greater among later-born children (Belmont, Stein, and Susser, 1975). Presumably, parents have less time to spend with each individual child as successive children are born. Thus, the explanation offered for the poorer scholastic performance of children in larger families seems applicable to ordinal birth position also. However, it is also possible that differences associated with ordinal position per se, rather than differences in family size, affect parent-child interaction. There is every reason to believe that children in different ordinal positions are treated differently by parents because of their position. For example, we would expect the methods of handling a second child to differ from those of handling the first because of experiences gained. Despite the expectations relating to the effects of ordinal birth position that this argument might appear to give rise to, studies in which the number of siblings have been held constant do not consistently provide evidence that ordinal position affects children's scholastic performance (Heer, 1985).

The "conflluence" model of Zajonc and his associates (Zajonc and Bargh, 1980; Zajonc and Markus, 1975; Zajonc, Markus, and Markus, 1979) was an attempt to explain differences in intellectual development that have been found to be associated with family size and, in some cases, with birth order in terms of the intellectual "level" of the home during the course of the child's development. The intellectual level is the average of the current intellectual ability of all family members (including parents and children) at any given time. According to the model, when an additional child is born, the average intellectual level of the family drops (since the newborn child's intellectual level is very low) and thus the general educational environment of the family is diminished. It is suggested that this has negative consequences for children's intellectual development. The model also helps to explain findings regarding the beneficial effects of spacing. The longer the time before a second child is born, the longer the first child has to grow in a more favorable intellectual environment. In this situation also, the intellectual environment of the family will be higher for the second child than if the interval between births had been shorter.

Although some research data (particularly aggregated data from large groups) support the confluence model, other data do not. One research finding that does not seem to fit the model is that only children have a lower level of general ability than children in two-sibling families: on the basis of the model, one would expect that the ability level of the only child would be highest of all. To explain the anomaly, Zajonc and Markus (1975) suggest that children with younger siblings adopt a teaching role within the family, something that the only child does not have the opportunity to do, and that this has positive consequences for their intellectual development. While this explanation seems plausible, we have very little information about sibling teaching that might support it (Scott-Jones, 1984).

Our understanding of the relationships between variables in family structure and children's scholastic abilities and achievements is obviously not very advanced. For example, the finding that the relationship between family size and school learning is more marked in lower socioeconomic classes (McGillicuddy-DeLisi, 1982) raises questions about how a variety of cultural factors might affect the nature of the relationship. In our present state of knowledge, we can only hazard guesses. It has been suggested, for example, that when religious belief excludes family limitation, the role of family size as a factor in influencing school learning may be removed. The suggestion, advanced by Floud, Halsey, and Martin (1957), arose from the finding that the usual negative relationship between family size and general scholastic ability did not exist for the Catholic families that they studied in Middlesbrough, England, where a proportionately greater number of children from large Catholic families than from large non-Catholic families gained admission to selective secondary grammar schools around the age of eleven. The inference, if justified in any circumstances, could hold only for children in the upper range of general ability, since only such children were selected for grammar schools. When, in a further study, the relationship between family size and verbal reasoning ability was examined in a predominantly Catholic population, the inference of Floud, Halsey, and Martin was not supported: the relationship between family size and reasoning ability was found to be negative as in other studies (Kellaghan and Macnamara, 1972).

The findings of some studies of the relationship between family size and scholastic performance that have been carried out in non-Western societies present a different picture, keeping alive the possibility that cultural factors may be important in considering how family size affects school-related abilities and achievements. In studies in Kenya (Bali, Drenth, van der Flier, and Young, 1984) and in Tanzania (Drenth, van der Flier, and Omari, 1983), a positive rather than a negative relationship was found between family size and educational achievement, measured in a variety of ways — standardized tests of ability and externally administered achievement examinations at primary and secondary levels. A similar finding has been reported for Indochinese refugee families living in the United States, for whom a positive relationship was found between family size and children's grade-point average. A possible explanation is that older children help younger ones with their homework. If this is so, then sibling involvement, when the culture promotes such involvement, may encourage and enhance school learning, offsetting the disadvantages often found in a large family (Caplan, Choy, and Whitmore, 1992).

The Role of Parental Characteristics

Parental characteristics, especially parents' attitudes to education, their interest in their children's education, and their beliefs in the value of schooling, have been found to be related to measures of children's scholastic behavior in several studies (Fraser, 1959; Great Britain: Department of Education and Science, 1967; Keeves, 1972; Marjoribanks, 1976). Such parental characteristics have been found to be more important than the actual material circumstances of homes.

In the large-scale survey of parents and schools carried out for the Central Advisory Council for Education (England), chaired by Lady Plowden, *Children and Their Primary Schools* (Great Britain: Department of Education and Science, 1967), variables were grouped into three categories: parent attitudes, home circumstances, and school factors. The first category centered on parents' hopeful and encouraging interest. Among the factors included under this heading were whether parents helped with the child's homework, whether the mother played with the child in the evening, whether the father took an interest in how his child was progressing in school, whether he did things with the child at weekends, whether he had been to the child's school and talked to the principal, and parents' educational aspirations for their child. The second category included parents' material circumstances (for example, physical amenities in the home) and the amount of education they had received. The third category was made up of various school circumstances. The results of the study indicated that more of the variation in children's school achievement could be accounted for by variation in parents' attitudes than by either variation in the material circumstances of homes or by variation in schools. Further, the relative importance of the parents' attitudes increased as the child grew older.

Although the investigators in this study had expected parents' attitudes, home circumstances, and schooling all to make a contribution to children's school achievement, they were surprised by the relative size of the contribution made by the parents' attitudes. However, the term *attitude* was used in a very broad sense and included a variety of social-psychological factors in the home (for example, mother playing with her child and helping with homework). When we consider the findings of studies of the relationship between such factors and the child's development in Chapter Four, the results of the Plowden investigation will not seem so surprising.

The findings of more recent studies of the performance of American students in national assessments in a variety of subject areas, including reading, writing, mathematics, and science, support the findings of earlier studies. These studies reveal consistent relationships between students' scholastic achievements and factors in the home such as parents' expectations, the availability of books and other reading materials, and the amount of attention the family gives to student schoolwork. The more encouragement and resources provided at home, the more likely students are to do well in school. Thus, it is concluded that "children are more likely to be successful learners if their parents or care-givers display an interest in what they are learning, provide access to learning materials, and serve as role models interested in their learning experiences" (Applebee, Langer, and Mullis, 1989, p. 34).

Conclusion

In this chapter, we reviewed the findings of studies that had examined relationships between home background, including parent characteristics, and children's scholastic performance. The findings are consistent across a large number of studies. Various indices of the status (parent income, parent occupation) and structure (family size, spacing between births) of families were found to be related to a variety of indices of children's school learning. However, the relationships are not strong.

A great many of the studies focused on the relationship between children's school performance and their social-class context and although it might be reasonable to expect this to affect the family learning environment experienced by children, the available evidence does not make clear the extent to which social status is an organizing force guiding relations between children's individual characteristics and school-related outcomes

(Marjoribanks, 1987). Further, while data on social class may provide a useful frame for a preliminary examination of such matters as incidence of single parents, mothers in the labor force, or remarriage (Bronfenbrenner, 1986), the information they provide is limited. Measures such as social class or socioeconomic status do not tell us "what the environment is like, what people are living there, what they are doing, or how the activities taking place could affect the child" (Bronfenbrenner and Crouter, 1982, pp. 361–362). In the next chapter, we will address this issue by considering the findings of studies that set out to identify activities in the home that are related to children's school learning.

FOUR ■ Home Processes
and School Learning

The research evidence on relationships between home background and children's school learning that we considered in Chapter Three was based on fairly crude indices of family conditions. Despite the many research studies using such indices, our understanding of the relationships between home background and scholastic ability and achievement remained limited. As we have seen, the explanatory value of such variables as parent occupation or education is limited, since they tell us relatively little about what goes on in homes that might affect children's scholastic development. Similarly, studies of parent characteristics, including attitudes, cannot provide us with a complete picture of the home. Like social-status variables, parent characteristics can tell us only a limited amount about how the home might contribute to children's school learning. Further information is needed that will tell us what people (especially parents) do and that will go some way toward capturing the complexity of the interactions between behavioral and environmental factors in the home.

Some of the studies that we considered in Chapter Three that sought to distinguish homes of different socioeconomic levels point to the importance of parent-child interactions. Studies of parent attitudes point in the same direction since they seem to include parent behaviors that might well be of much greater consequence for children's scholastic development than the actual attitudes.

50

The confluence model proposed by Zajonc and his associates (Zajonc and Bargh, 1980; Zajonc and Markus, 1975; Zajonc, Markus, and Markus, 1979) also went some way toward explaining how such factors as family size, birth position, and space between births might affect intellectual development through their influence on the intellectual environment of the home. But the model does not identify the characteristics of the intellectual environment that might affect children's development nor how they might operate. Neither can it explain why family size seems to have more effect on development in families of low socioeconomic status than in families of high status.

Such considerations have led to attempts by a number of investigators to identify and describe aspects of the "curriculum" and of "teaching styles" in homes that might account for differences in children's preparation for and guidance through the learning tasks of school. Although there are early examples of this kind of study (for example, Burks, 1928), it was not until much later that extensive work in the area commenced. The aim of investigators was to identify processes within the larger network of family interactions that are relevant to the development of particular characteristics in children, such as verbal ability, achievement in school subjects, motivation, and self-esteem. The word "process" is used in this context to describe a variety of activities in the home that are considered to play an important role in children's development: how time and space are organized and used, how parents and children interact and spend their time, and the values that govern parents' and children's choice of activities. It is these things rather than the social or socioeconomic status of parents that determine how well children do at school.

The focus of many studies that investigated these aspects of homes tended to be fairly specific, focusing on a single aspect of the home, for example the extent of provision for general learning, the emphasis on language development, the type of educational stimulation provided, or the general degree of concern for learning and achievement. We will look briefly at the main findings of studies that used such individual variables before we consider studies that used a more integrated approach in their description of the conditions in the home that affect school learning. We will find that the more specific studies provide evidence that serves to underline the relevance and importance of the variables included in the more integrated approach.

Findings of Home Process Studies

The findings of the large number of studies that focused on particular variables related to or implying home processes may be summarized briefly. First, in a number of studies, children's high scholastic achievement was found to be associated with high academic expectations and aspirations on the parts of parents (Gordon, Olmsted, Robin, and True, 1979; Great Britain: Department of Education and Science, 1967; Keeves, 1975). Such expectations and aspirations can be regarded as constituting pressure on children to achieve at school.

Second, the findings of many studies underline the importance of the language environment of the home. In these studies, the use of complex levels and styles of language and thought in interaction with children was found to be associated with high achievement in children. Verbal variety and the use of detailed instruction and of advanced organizing information were found to be features of such language (Gordon, 1973; Hess and Shipman, 1965; Olmsted and Jester, 1972).

Third, evidence supporting the importance of academic guidance and support in the home comes from several studies that found that achievement in children is associated with the parents' use of appropriate teaching modes and strategies when children are young and their provision of a high level of academic guidance when children got older. Further, the parents of high-achieving children were found to be closely attuned to the cognitive level of their children and to be likely to respond more to cues provided by the children than to preconceived expectations or status rules for the children (Brophy, 1970; Hess and Shipman, 1965; Schaefer, 1972).

Fourth, stimulation in the home, as represented by opportunities provided by parents for children to explore ideas, events, and the larger environment, was found to be important for children's scholastic development. In Chapter Three, we saw how parents vary in the way they treat children's questions and in the extent to which they encourage children to explore the meaning of events. This variation has important implications for children's development. So also has parent involvement with children in a variety of activities, apart from ones with direct scholastic implications. Thus, for example, children whose mothers spend time with them in the evenings, playing or reading or taking them out, have an advantage at school (Great Britain: Department of Education and Science, 1967). Parents' assistance in the development of problem-solving strategies is also associated with high scholastic achievement (Hess and Shipman, 1965; Olmsted and Jester, 1972).

Finally, the general work habits of the family seem relevant to children's intellectual development. Children are more likely to perform well at school if there is structure in the management of the home and if parents express a preference for educational activities when choice exists (Bradley, Caldwell, and Elardo, 1977).

Toward a Comprehensive Model of the Home

Some attempts to describe the characteristics of homes that are related to school learning adopted a more comprehensive view of the home environment, in effect encompassing all the factors considered in the last section, to create a home process model. The prototype for these studies can be found in work carried out at the University of Chicago in the early 1960s. Its aim was to provide a comprehensive picture of processes in the home that would represent what parents do with their children that promotes school learning (Bloom, 1964; Davé, 1963; Wolf, 1964, 1966). Bloom (1981) has categorized the variables under five major headings: *work habits of the family* (covering degree of structure and routine in home management and preference for educational activities over other activities); *academic guidance and support* (relating to guidance on school matters and the availability and use of materials and facilities for school learning); *stimulation to explore and discuss ideas and events* (which can be inferred

The five home variables discussed here and in Chapter Nine are from B.S. Bloom, *All Our Children Learning: A Primer for Parents, Teachers, and Other Educators* (New York: McGraw-Hill, 1981). Reprinted with permission of McGraw-Hill.

from the family's choice of hobbies, games, and other activities and the opportunities it provides for thinking and imagination); *language environment* (which relates to language modeling and opportunities provided for correct and effective use of language); and *academic aspirations and expectations* (covering not only aspirations and expectations but also knowledge of the educational progress of the child, standards of reward for scholastic achievement, and preparation and planning for the attainment of educational goals). More detail on these variables is provided in Chapter Nine.

Studies using measures of home process variables have been carried out in a variety of countries since the early 1960s (see Iverson and Walberg, 1982; Kalinowski and Sloane, 1981; Marjoribanks, 1979a, 1979b). In most of the studies, the variables related to measures of scholastic ability or achievement, but some examined relationships between family variables and students' personality and affective characteristics. What is perhaps remarkable is that the home process variables have been useful in describing homes in a variety of cultural contexts and that variance between homes in the variables is related to children's school learning in non-Western societies as well as in Western societies. It would seem that, even in homes that differ from each other in a great variety of ways, home processes represent aspects of the family environment that are significant for success in the formal educational system.

Home Processes and Cognitive Development

In most of the studies of cogitive development, standardized tests of achievement were used. In some studies, general ability or verbal ability was examined, using either an individually administered test (for example, the Stanford-Binet Intelligence Scale or the Wechsler Intelligence Scale for Children) or a group-administered test (for example, the Lorge Thorndike Intelligence Test or the Primary Mental Abilities Test). A number of studies set out to relate home processes to different aspects of scholastic ability — for example, to verbal ability, to reading achievement, and to arithmetic achievement (Kellaghan, 1977a; Linnan,

1976). When school achievement was studied, a variety of standardized tests (for example, the Iowa Test of Basic Skills), as well as marks in academic courses (focusing for the most part on achievement in reading and mathematics) were used.

A number of general conclusions may be drawn from these studies. Measures of process variables in the home predict scholastic ability and achievement better than do measures of social class, family structure, or parental characteristics. While studies of the relationship between social class and scholastic ability and achievement yield correlations of between .2 and .5, the correlation between home process measures and ability (Henmon-Nelson Test) has been found to be .70 (Wolf, 1964). Correlations between home process measures and performance on subtests of the Metropolitan Achievement Tests ranged from .56 for arithmetic computation to .79 for word knowledge (Davé, 1963). These findings confirm the view that what parents *do* is more important than what they *are*.

The findings also indicate that there is considerable variation in family environments within a social class, a conclusion that is supported by the findings of studies in which the range of social class was limited. For example, Greaney and Hegarty (1987), who worked in a middle-class area, and Kellaghan (1977a), who worked in a disadvantaged area, found significant relationships between home process variables and scholastic ability and achievement. As one would expect, the magnitude of the relationship was not as large in these studies as in studies that were based on samples of the general population. There is some evidence that the relationship between home processes and school learning may be stronger for students from middle socioeconomic backgrounds than for students from lower socioeconomic backgrounds (Iverson and Walberg, 1982).

Although home process variables predict scholastic ability and achievement better than does social class, they are not unrelated to the home's socioeconomic status. Homes that are classified as high in social status are likely to be treated higher on home process variables than are homes classified as low in social status. Important questions that arise from this observation are whether the characteristics described by the home process variables can be altered, particularly in homes that might generally be described as disadvantaged; and if they can, whether that would have an effect on children's school learning (see Bloom, 1981). These questions are addressed in Chapter Seven.

Not only has the description of homes in terms of processes been found useful among different socioeconomic groups, it has worked well in a variety of other environmental conditions. It has been found useful in predicting achievement in urban environments (Davé, 1963; Wolf, 1964) and in rural ones (McGurk, 1973), inside the United States and outside the United States, in other Western countries—for example, in Ireland (Fitzgerald, 1975; Greaney and Hegarty, 1987; Kellaghan, 1977a, 1977b)—and in developing countries—in Trinidad (Dyer, 1967), in Thailand (Janhom, 1983), and in Indonesia (Johnstone and Jiyono, 1983).

Linnan (1976) explored an interesting issue in the light of research indicating that patterns of ability differ for different ethnic groups (Lesser, Fifer, and Clark, 1965; Stodolsky and Lesser, 1967). In a search for differences in home environments that might account for differences in patterns of ability, Linnan examined relationships between home process variables and three cognitive abilities (spatial, reasoning, and verbal, as measured by the Primary Mental Abilities Test) in two communities living in urban areas in the United States, one predominantly Jewish, the other predominantly Irish. Although the study found that mental ability scores were related to ethnic background, as in the Lesser studies, there was no evidence that the pattern of home processes in the community of the ethnic groups was responsible for the ethnically unique patterns of score. In fact, social class was more closely associated with home process variables than was ethnicity.

A question related to that posed by Linnan, and one that has frequently been raised in examining the role of the home in children's development, is whether particular patterns of home processes operate selectively to develop certain abilities and to leave others relatively underdeveloped (Walberg and Marjoribanks, 1976). A clear answer to this question does not emerge from the studies we reviewed, partly because analytic procedures that might have thrown light on the issue were constrained by the small number of parents and children in many of the studies (see Rankin, 1981). However, across studies relating home process variables to both general scholastic ability and achievement, the evidence consistently indicates that home processes are more strongly related to some children's abilities and achievements than to others. First, home process variables correlate more highly with measures of verbal ability, or what has been called "crystallized intelligence," than with measures of nonverbal ability, such as spatial ability or what has been called "fluid intelligence" (Kellaghan, 1977a; Linnan, 1976; Marjoribanks, 1974b; Walberg and Marjoribanks, 1973). Second, home process variables are more closely related to measures of scholastic achievement, particularly in the basic school subjects of reading and mathematics, than to measures of general scholastic or verbal ability (Fitzgerald, 1975; Iverson and Walberg, 1982; Kellaghan, 1977a). Third, there is some evidence that within the area of scholastic achievement, home process variables are more closely related to general areas of achievement than to more specialized (and presumably more school-based) areas, such as science (Keeves, 1974). In general, these conclusions are consistent with the findings of studies that used status measures (for example, social class) to classify home environments (for example, Eells and others, 1951; Marjoribanks, 1974b; Walberg and Marjoribanks, 1973).

The findings point to a number of conclusions that serve to underline the importance and explicate the nature of home environments in school learning. First, the finding that all the cognitive characteristics in children that have been investigated are related to variance in home conditions points to the pervasiveness of home influences on development. Second, although home factors are related to all aspects of development, their contribution seems to vary from one cognitive characteristic to another. It is of particular interest that areas of development closely related to schoolwork (reading, mathematics) are sensitive to the influence of the home. Since reading and mathematics are not normally taught at home, it follows that what must be important for successful school learning are general conditions of learning in the home, comprising the structural, behavioral, and attitudinal factors that were assessed in the studies described in this chapter.

Since children's needs and capabilities change as they develop, as do their interactions with their parents (Scott-Jones, 1984), we might expect home processes to have a different impact at different stages of the child's development. Though sufficient comparable studies have not been carried out that would allow us to accurately chart the influence of home processes as the child develops, there is some evidence that the relationship between home environment and school achievement is slightly closer for older children (Iverson and Walberg, 1982). However, the problem of measuring achievement in young children has to be recognized in reaching this conclusion.

Home Processes and Personality Development

Process variables have also been used in studies in which the main interest was the noncognitive characteristics of children, though these studies have been much fewer in number than studies that examined the relationships between home process variables and cognitive outcomes. Noncognitive characteristics that have received attention include motivation for achievement, self-esteem (Weiss, 1974), self-concept of ability, attitudes to school (Marjoribanks, 1978), and indices of mental health (Dolan, 1980). Outcomes were measured by self-report questionnaires, teacher ratings, and projective techniques.

Studies of noncognitive characteristics are of interest for at least two reasons. First, a consideration of the development of such characteristics as children's conceptions of self and their attitudes, values, and habits underlines the importance of the home, since it is in the home, to a degree that is not possible in the school, that these attributes are fostered through personal attention and interest, intimacy, intensity of involvement, and persistence and continuity over time. And second, noncognitive development is important for the more cognitively oriented work of the school, since in its absence, it would appear that schools are not likely to be very successful in helping students master the scholastic tasks they will face (Academic Development Institute, 1989; Coleman, 1987, 1990; Redding, 1991).

One would not necessarily expect the home processes that contribute to noncognitive development to be the same as those that affect cognitive development. With this in mind—and on the basis of a review of the theoretical and empirical literature in the areas of child development, motivation, and socialization— Weiss (1974) identified two sets of process variables that he expected would affect each of two outcomes of interest in his study (achievement motivation and self-concept). Although the variables identified are not the same as those identified in the studies of cognitive achievement, there is some overlap. The network for achievement motivation consisted of the *generation of standards of excellence and expectations* (levels of parental aspiration and competitiveness, risk taking, and work habits), *independence training* (freedom and aid given to children), and *parental approval* (involvement in, awareness of, and approval given to children's activities). The network for self-esteem included *parental acceptance* (involvement in, awareness of, and acceptance of children's activities, evaluation of children's competencies and characteristics) and *opportunities for self-enhancement* (extent of privacy, encouragement to explore new things, and children's involvement in decision making).

Studies have been less successful in establishing relationships between the home environment and noncognitive development than between the home environment and cognitive development. While Weiss (1974) found moderately high correlations (over .50) between home process variables and personality characteristics, other investigators have not (for example, Marjoribanks, 1978). This finding may be attributed, in part at any rate, to the difficulty of establishing the validity of criterion instruments for personality characteristics.

Conclusion

In this chapter, we considered studies that had constructed more or less elaborate models to represent the complex patterns of behavior that undoubtedly characterize children's experience in

the family. The high degree of relationship between home processes and scholastic performance that was found in the studies
can be taken as evidence that aspects of the home environment
crucial for the child's development are being tapped. The consistency with which such relationships have been recorded in
a variety of socioeconomic and cultural circumstances adds to
one's confidence in the validity of the model of the home environment that guided the empirical investigations.

    This is not to claim that, despite its high predictive value,
the home process model provides us with a description of the
home that is entirely comprehensive or sufficiently detailed in
its analysis of the complex dynamics of family relationships.
While it is reasonable to conclude that it does provide an overall description of the processes in the home that are related to
performance in school, it does not allow us to distinguish between the contributions of different members of the family or
how those members interact in constructing the processes or in
their operation. For example, in using the model, it is easy to
lose sight of the fact that children influence their parents as well
as parents their children. Although it is true that parents provide the overall context for the growth of their children, it is
also a fact that this context can be modified by the reactions
of the children and that parents are influenced by children's characteristics and behavior in applying child-rearing strategies
(Scott-Jones, 1984). This situation is illustrated in two descriptions by investigators using an interview schedule to assess home
process variables in research studies. In one study, Hanson
(1975) noted that not all children react the same when parents
read to them: some would ask for more, while others would resist
by refusing to sit still, by making noise, or by being generally
inattentive. Linnan (1976) went further when he noted the extent to which parents' behavior seemed to be modified by their
children's interests. For example, one mother he interviewed
responded to her child's interest in reading by providing additional books, while another, also in response to a child's interest,
provided family excursions. Other factors that seem relevant
in the study of home-school relationships are the structure of
the family, the role of the father as well as of the mother, the

roles of brothers, sisters, and other family members, and the gender of the child.

The complexity of the family that these factors highlight should make us cautious in drawing inferences about causality from the studies that have been carried out. The vast majority of studies of the relationship between home environment (however measured) and children's scholastic development have been correlational in character. While it is true that the selection of variables to be included in descriptions of homes received a good deal of thought and was usually based on a conceptual analysis of the situation and the findings of earlier research, the fact remains that the findings of correlational research cannot form the basis of unequivocal conclusions about cause-effect relationships. If it were possible to use an experimental design, it would reduce uncertainty in making causal inferences; but for practical and ethical reasons, such a procedure is not normally possible. One approach is available, however, that would help to support causal interpretations of the data reviewed in this chapter. It would involve attempting to alter the behavior of parents and then, using an experimental or quasi-experimental design, examining the effects of the parents' altered behavior on the scholastic development of their children. In Chapter Seven, we shall see that when this approach is adopted changes ensue in the home that are matched by improvements in children's school performance, strongly supporting the view that the home processes identified in this chapter are causally related to school achievement.

FIVE ◼ Changes in Society and the Family

In the studies reviewed in Chapters Three and Four, which established relationships between home factors and school learning, it was assumed for the most part that homes were inhabited by nuclear families, made up of children and two parents, one of whom worked outside the home. The studies did not distinguish between such homes and ones in which the family did not conform to this traditional structure. Neither did they usually take into account the impact on families and children's education of the community and the neighborhood or of a range of changes that are taking place in society — factors such as increasing urbanization and migration, changes in the labor force, growth in technology, growth in knowledge and information, and a movement toward decentralization. It is to these changes and their implications for family functioning that we turn in this chapter. We also consider the implications for children's development and education of a variety of inceasingly common family conditions: families with working parents, one-parent families, blended families, and families in which the culture differs from the mainstream culture.

At the outset, we recognize that the complexity of communities and neighborhoods makes it difficult to isolate the particular features of a community or neighborhood that might affect behavior (Mayer and Jencks, 1989). Neighborhood institutions and resources form one possible source of influence.

62

Thus, the quality of the local school might be expected to have some effect on how much students learn, while the presence or absence of other institutions, such as a church or scout patrol, might be expected to relate to young people's behavior.

As well as institutions, individuals in the community may also affect young people's behavior. For example, individuals can provide models of behavior that encourage young people to stay in school or to avoid delinquent acts. They can also support and control children's behavior, keeping them from running wild on the streets or protecting them if they are in danger.

Although we would expect communities and immediate neighbors to influence families in their behavior and values, we have to recognize that families and individuals also hold values, on the basis of which they make choices that may not reflect the values of those around them. Thus, in communities that value formal education, it is not unusual to find individuals who do not do well at school, just as one also finds in communities that do not seem to place a high value on formal education people who do well in the educational system. Indeed, though material resources and social relationships in a community are related to student achievement, they seem to be much less important than the characteristics of individual students and families (Hoffer and Coleman, 1990).

Changes in Society

Formal educational facilities were initially provided on the assumption that earlier educational and more general development needs would continue to be met in the home and in the community. Recently, Coleman (1987, 1990) has outlined the conditions in the home and in the community that he considers to be necessary to meet those educational and developmental needs and has described how the conditions are being eroded in contemporary society. According to Coleman, it is important for children's development that "social capital" in the form of norms and social networks, involving relationships between adults and children, be available in the child's home and community, since it is in such networks that people develop shared aspirations, provide mutual aid and support, especially in time of need, exchange information, define and uphold standards, and learn how to make use of community resources. In turn, these conditions contribute to the development in children of basic attachments, attitudes, a willingness to make certain efforts, and concepts of self-esteem, all of which work to children's advantage when they go to school. A variety of individuals and organizations can help children with these developmental tasks — older siblings, grandparents and other members of the extended family, neighbors, church organizations, and various social and cultural groups.

Although the Age of Reason and the Industrial Revolution may have brought some benefits for families, such as the psychological intensification of the family circle as well as formal schooling (Ariés, 1973; Barker-Benfield, 1992), at the same time, seeds were being sown by other developments associated with the Industrial Revolution that would have the effect of undermining many traditional community and family support networks (see Coleman, 1987, 1990; Comer, 1984). Although the great variations that exist between countries always render it hazardous to generalize about global social trends, it is possible in most regions of the world today to identify changes, some of which began with the Industrial Revolution, that are adversely affecting family life. The most significant of these changes, which we will now consider, are the growth of urban centers and of migration; changes in the labor force, in working environments, and in particular, in the role of women in society; the increasing presence of modern technology in almost every area of life, including the home; the growing importance of knowledge and information; and the movement toward decentralization of social services and administration, which is accompanied by a return to local groups, families, and individuals of responsibilities they once had.

Urbanization and Migration

Twenty-five years ago there were only 150 cities in the world with a population of over 500,000; today there are approximately

500. In industrialized countries, about 75 percent of inhabitants live in urban areas; the developing nations, particularly middle-income ones, are increasingly moving toward this situation. When societies create urban conglomerates, not only do they alter the natural landscape, they also change the cultural and social relations of the people who live there. Family organization and habits may be affected in various ways. Generally, less space is available for family life and household size tends to decrease. More time is spent in daily travel from home to work, to school, and to other places, limiting time for interactions between family members. Not all of these trends are consistent. Living in a large urban area, for example, does not always mean living in a small household. As a result of the recent economic crisis in several Latin American countries, extended families are again becoming common in cities (Raczynski, 1986). Furthermore, a noticeable trend to migrate from large metropolitan areas to small towns has been observed in France, Great Britain, and the United States. Nowadays, migration in one form or another—from a rural area to a city, from a city to a small town, from a poor and politically unstable country to a neighboring state—is a common experience for many children.

Prior to this century, when population mobility was limited, the stability of households and the fact that personal relationships grew in relatively well-defined small communities diminished the likelihood of conflict between families and schools and between these institutions and society at large. Although urbanization and migration do not mean that community ceases to exist, they do often mean that adults' circles of relationships are less likely to include parents of their children's associates, thus cutting off opportunities to know what their children are doing and to influence their children's actions through norms and sanctions (Hoffer and Coleman, 1990). Further, families that do not have the opportunities and spaces to meet, talk, and exchange opinions often drift into feelings of isolation and rootlessness (van Leer Foundation, 1988).

Some characteristics of the physical environment surrounding the family can adversely affect children's intellectual development. Overstimulation, a crowded home, excessive noise, lack of personal space to study, and other factors associated with life in urban settings can all negatively affect behavior and school performance (Scott-Jones, 1984). So too can marital discord and weak family relationships, factors also associated with urban living, which have been found in Britain to be related to a higher incidence of psychiatric disturbance and social deviance in children (Rutter, 1985a).

On a more positive note, urban families are likely to have access to better social services and educational facilities and to a wider range of jobs. New options for leisure time become available and the city can offer, for some children at any rate, a rich and differentiated cultural environment that includes libraries, museums, and theaters. All of these can provide opportunities for permanent informal education, including the formation of attitudes and values. In one Swiss study, a significant positive relationship was found between richness of the community environment and children's mental test scores (Vatter, 1981). Of course, not all urban environments provide rich cultural environments or, if they do, young people do not use them. The urban environment can be as bleak as it is rich.

Changes in the Labor Force

The industrialization process that began three centuries ago in Great Britain has influenced to a greater or lesser extent all other nations. Its most obvious effect, perhaps, in addition to the migration of vast numbers of people from rural to urban areas, has been the creation of a variety of skilled and partly skilled occupations to replace the work of the farm. The effects of industrialization on society, however, go far beyond a restructuring of the labor force. Industrialization has also led to the evolution of trade systems, the advance of technology, flexibility in personal relationships, and ultimately, significant reorganization of society as a whole and changes in people's attitudes and ideologies. In the sphere of education, it has resulted in a demand for specialization and the development of technical and technological skills and attitudes.

Of course, social attitudes and ideologies take a long time

to change, especially when they affect intimate human relationships such as those found in the family. In the evolution of attitudes and ideologies, old and new values and attitudes can coexist in a variety of ways. For example, in a study of male factory workers in six countries (Argentina, Bangladesh, Chile, India, Israel, and Nigeria) during the course of regional industrialization, two distinct ideologies were found among the workers: belief in independence from the extended family and belief in women's rights outside the home but not necessarily inside it (Karen, 1984).

In the rural areas of many developing countries, the family today is still the main productive unit and children's work typically forms a large component of this unit. In rural Columbia, for example, children's work represents about 16 percent of family income (Ramirez, 1987). In this situation, study and work become complementary activities in the overall socialization process of children. The informal economy, which is growing in many cities of middle- and low-income countries, is also often based on the work of the family. Children may contribute to this work, as they do in rural areas, but their involvement is likely to be less than that of rural children.

In developed economies, many more people are engaged in the industrial and service sectors than in agriculture, and children are more removed from the world of work. Productive activity is no longer primarily centered in the family home, while the workplace is becoming the locus of many activities other than just work; in many cases, it plays an important role in people's social and political learning as well as affecting family function and structure. While research does not provide unambiguous findings on how a parent's occupation might affect child-rearing attitudes and practices, it does suggest some interesting relationships. For example, there is evidence that fathers' job-related experiences affect the quality of father-child interactions, which in turn affect children's behavior (Barling, 1991). As we saw in Chapter Three, there is also evidence that the structure and content of activities in a father's job are somehow translated into family child-rearing values. Thus, fathers in jobs that require compliance with authority have been found to tend to stress obedience in their children, while fathers in jobs that require self-direction and independence expect similar characteristics in their children (Bronfenbrenner, 1986).

The growing participation of women in the labor force is a well-documented world trend (Coleman, 1990). In industrialized countries, the female share of the labor force today is in many places close to that of the male. It is particularly high (close to 50 percent) in Scandinavian countries and in the United States. Female participation in the labor force, however, is not confined to industrialized countries and is also quite high in many traditional economies. In particular, the female share of agricultural employment, either in a paid or unpaid capacity, is substantial, reaching over 40 percent in several African countries (Botswana, Ghana, Lesotho, Malawi, and Rwanda) (International Labour Organization, 1985). While these figures might suggest that women now have greater opportunities to choose from among different activities in the family and the economy, in practice, they may have no real choice; and whether or not they have choice, their involvement in work outside the home is not always accompanied by appropriate means of social support.

Many women in paid employment are married or are mothers of preschool children, and their proportion in the workforce is also increasing, particularly in Europe and the United States. In the United States, the number of women with children under the age of six who were employed increased from 2.3 million in 1960 to 7.1 million in 1988. Further, recent statistics indicate that half of the mothers with infants who are one year old or less and almost two-thirds of the mothers with children aged two and three years are in the workforce. Although percentages are higher for married mothers and for mothers with fewer children, the percentages for all subgroups are over 50 (Baydar and Brooks-Gunn, 1991).

As one would expect, changes in the composition of the labor force and in the role of women in society have had direct effects on the structure and functioning of families. They have affected, for example, the age at which couples establish a family and the number of children they have. They have also affected the style and intensity of relationships among family members and the amount of time that parents can give to children.

Growth in Technology

New technologies are everywhere influencing people's life-styles and their interpersonal relationships. In the home, they can free women from domestic chores, allowing them to spend more time with their children. However, they can also absorb children's time, interfering with and limiting opportunities for richer human exchanges.

Of all the new technologies, television is the one that has had the greatest impact on how people spend their time. Television viewing is one of the most popular entertainments among children throughout the world. Statistics from the United States indicate that more than 95 percent of households have a television set that is turned on, on average, for about seven hours a day, and is watched by children between the ages of six and eleven for approximately twenty-seven hours per week (Dorr, 1986). In other countries also (for example, Spain, New Zealand, and Venezuela), large numbers of nine-year-olds watch TV for more than five hours a day (Elley, 1992). Age is strongly related to television viewing: viewing increases from childhood to a peak in early adolescence, after which it declines. Children from disadvantaged backgrounds spend more time watching television than children from more affluent homes.

Research findings suggest that children's information, attitudes, and behavior are influenced by what they see on television. The relationship between amount of time spent watching television and school performance, however, appears to be modest. For example, in the United States, higher levels of television viewing have been found to be associated with slightly lower grades at school (Dornbush, 1986). In international studies of achievement, heavy television viewing has been found to be related to somewhat lower achievement in science and mathematics in Canada, Ireland, South Korea, Spain, the United States, and the United Kingdom (Lapointe, Mead, and Phillips, 1988) and to lower reading achievement in Belgium, Denmark,

France, Germany, Ireland, New Zealand, Switzerland, and the United States (Elley, 1992). Small amounts of viewing, however, may be beneficial: children who spend less than ten hours a week watching television tend to do better at school than children who watch no television at all. In some social contexts, moderately heavy television has been found to be positively related to reading achievement. The explanation for this may lie in the fact that the presence of television may be an indicator of higher socioeconomic status in developing countries.

It is clear that there are positive and negative aspects to television. On the negative side, it can be argued that much television is "aggressive, sexist, ageist, racist, consumption oriented, sexy, inane, or moronic" (Dorr, 1986, p. 82). On the positive side, in a realistic and interesting way, television provides information about the physical, social, and spiritual world that interests children (Dorr, 1986). It can be used to provide reassuring background noise and companionship as well as conversational topics and opportunities for physical and emotional contact (Lull, 1980). A study in the city of Santiago de Chile provides examples of both positive and negative effects. In the study, 65 percent of people said that they usually viewed television with the family; however, they did not consider that television helped family unity (CENECA, FLASCO, 1987).

The microcomputer is another potentially influential instructional device, both in the home and in the school. Sales of computers for family use increased in most countries for several years. However, research on the impact of microcomputers on school achievement has produced evidence that is mixed and conflicting (Papagiannis, Douglas, Williamson, and Le Mon, 1987). It would appear that children who have microcomputers at home do not generally use them for academic or learning purposes, preferring to play electronic games—which, of course, compete with other family activities (Giaquinta and Ely, 1986). It is clear that parents will have to compensate for technologies by intensifying care and family relationships. As in the case of television, computers can play a role in this by serving as a focus for family discussion and exchange. The main issue would seem not to be the presence of technology, but how it can best be managed to improve human relationships and education.

Growth in Knowledge and Information

One of the positive aspects of recent scientific and technological development is the increase in the availability of vast amounts of knowledge for many people. However, the information is not equally available to all. Indeed, one of the major differences between, for example, an urban middle-class family and an isolated rural family lies in their differential ability to access information and to use it.

The continual expansion of knowledge is a constant challenge to schools, since it implies the need to update curricula. A negative consequence of this is that parents may find it increasingly difficult to help their children with their schoolwork. Thus, new approaches and the teaching of new content in schools may have the effect of widening the gap between school and home. This will be most evident for homes that do not have the resources to keep up with new developments.

Movement Toward Decentralization

The development of welfare systems in many industrialized countries has increased government responsibility for child care and education to such an extent that concern has been expressed about the long-term social effects of the decreasing role of parents in the education of new generations. At the same time, there is also concern in countries such as the United States that changes in the population structure (especially the increase in the number of older people) and in the provision of social services designed to improve the well-being of the elderly will result in a deterioration of services for young people (Preston, 1984). There is a danger that formal educational institutions for children will receive fewer resources at a time when more is being expected of them as the roles of other institutions in children's education decrease.

The underfunding of education is not helped by the fact

that rates of economic growth are slowing in developed countries, while economic adjustment and social changes are taking place in developing ones. In the developing countries in particular, the need to reduce public investment and to increase the contributions of other sectors of society is focusing public attention on such issues as the participation of families and communities in local government and in the management of social services, mainly education. The move to decentralization, already underway in many parts of the world, inevitably raises questions about how the family fits into this movement and how it can be assisted to increase the unique input it can have in children's education.

Changes in the Family

Evidence from traditional as well as from modern societies suggests that although the basic socializing institution, the family, still remains a solid social entity, it is changing in its structure, functions, and internal dynamics more rapidly and more radically than it ever did in the past. Indeed, the changes have been so radical that today's family is very little like the "traditional" family of yesterday (Coleman, 1987, 1990; Hoffer and Coleman, 1990). The role of the family as an important and valued basic social institution is being affected not only by the societal changes we have just considered but also by the fact that two of its main supports, marriage and fertility, are under pressure, while two of its traditional functions, socialization and production, are being shared by other institutions.

In the Western world, registered marriages are declining, while separation and divorce rates are increasing. For example, between 1972 and 1985, the number of registered marriages in France declined from 416,000 to 273,000, while the number of divorces increased from 43,000 to 109,600. At the same time, fertility rates are decreasing worldwide (except in some countries, especially in Sub-Saharan Africa). The lowest fertility rates are found among industrial-market economies where, with some exceptions, total fertility rates are at or below the replacement level (two births per woman) (World Bank, 1978–1987).

While there have been changes in customs and attitudes

relating to marriage and the family, the most noticeable trans-
formations relate to family composition and structure, which
are changing profoundly. Household size is shrinking in most
high- and middle-income countries of the world, even in societies where extended family households existed for centuries.
Although the traditional ideal household in Japan is composed
of two married couples of different generations, an increasing
proportion of households is composed of a single family or of
a single individual parent (Martin and Culter, 1983). Similar
trends have been reported for the United States, where 63.4 percent of families have three members or less and the number of
people living alone rose from 10.9 million in 1970 to 20.6 million in 1985. Even in France, which has a long tradition of family
cohesiveness, 40 percent of families had only one chlid and one
household in four contained only one person in 1982. Fertility
in urban areas is lower than in rural areas and urban people
are motivated to delay or limit their childbearing to increase
their income (World Bank, 1984). The trend toward smaller
families is also to be found in low-income countries. China, for
example, has experienced remarkable changes since its 1949
revolution, so that Chinese families are now smaller, and fewer
are extended. It would appear that different generations now
live together only in cases of economic emergency (Yi, 1986).

One implication of the changes in patterns of family structure and of the emergence of new varieties of living arrangements is that it is becoming increasingly difficult to describe a
typical family model, if indeed it ever was possible. Family
households have always been very adaptable, but it is also evident that some current changes in the family can create specific
problems for children's development, including their school
learning. These relate to working parents, one-parent families,
blended families, and families in which the parents come from
a cultural background that differs from that of the culturally
mainstream school.

Working-Parent Families

At first blush, the consequences of both parents working would
appear to be two-edged. On the one hand, parental employment

should result in greater availability of material benefits. On the other hand, parents who work will have less time to spend with their children and, as a result, children might suffer in their psychological development. Some parents may regard child rearing as an impediment in the pursuit of their adult lives and expect the school to take total responsibility for their children's education (Coleman and Husén, 1985).

Whatever the consequences, the reality is that families in which both parents work are becoming increasingly common. This phenomenon has resulted in changes in many traditional "family management" arrangements; in particular, it involves a greater sharing of domestic activities among parents and children. Unfortunately, even with such sharing, it is often the case that parents do not have time to become fully involved in their children's formal schooling (for example, in homework and parent-teacher meetings) or in more general informal learning situations in the home. Initially, day-care centers and preschools were seen as solutions to this problem. Now, it looks as if there may be a need for extended extra-school and/or holiday programs as well (Coleman, 1987).

There are many factors that need to be considered when attempting to determine whether maternal work has an effect on the development of children and adolescents. These include the age of the child when the mother is working outside the family, the amount of time she spends outside the home, her educational level, the child's gender and temperament, characteristics of the child's family (structure, income, and support system), maternal-role satisfaction, father involvement, the quality of family interactions, and the availability, type, and quality of arrangements to look after the child in the mother's absence (Baydar and Brooks-Gunn, 1991; Chase-Landsdale, Michael, and Desai, 1991; Richards and Duckett, 1991; Zaslow, Rabinovich, and Suwalsky, 1991).

It is difficult to design research that will isolate the effects of maternal employment as distinct from the effects of the many conditions often associated with it. As a result, evidence regarding effects is limited and not always consistent (Chase-Landsdale, Michael, and Desai, 1991; Gottfried and Gottfried, 1988; Lerner and Galambos, 1991; Richards and Duckett, 1991). This absence of consistency has left much room for controversy regarding the impact of maternal employment on a variety of aspects of children's development, including socioeconomic, cognitive, language, motivation, and sex-role development.

    At present, the available research findings, though limited, point in a number of directions. First, the findings of many studies indicate that maternal employment per se need not have contemporaneous or long-term effects that are detrimental for children (Gottfried and Gottfried, 1988). Second, there is some support for the view that the age of the child during the mother's employment may be of some significance. It would not seem unreasonable to expect that maternal absence during early childhood might have negative effects, whereas absence during adolescence, when the individual is becoming increasingly independent, might be a very different experience, for both adolescent and mother (Richards and Duckett, 1991). In fact, research is helping to define more precisely the effects of maternal absence at different periods in children's lives. In a large-scale longitudinal study, Baydar and Brooks-Gunn (1991) found that maternal employment during the first year of life had negative effects on children's development, assessed when the children were three or four years of age. These effects were found for both cognitive development (assessed on a test of vocabulary) and behavioral development (assessed on a checklist of behavior problems, covering antisocial, anxious, depressed, and headstrong behavior, hyperactivity, immature dependency, and peer conflict–social withdrawal). The effects were similar for boys and girls and whether or not the child's family was considered to live in poverty. When maternal employment was postponed to the second or third years of a child's life, however, the effects on the child's cognitive and behavioral development were negligible.

    Whether maternal employment affects boys and girls differently is not clear from the available research evidence. Although many studies indicate that maternal employment does not have different consequences for boys and girls (Gottfried and Gottfried, 1988), some suggest that the effect on boys may be more negative. For example, negative effects have been reported in relation to socioemotional and cognitive development, school achievement, overall adjustment, and a tendency to develop insecure attachments to their mothers. Not only do girls not exhibit these negative reactions, they may benefit from mothers' employment. For example, adolescent daughters of employed mothers have been found to be more independent, better adjusted, and to have a more positive concept of the female role than daughters of mothers who did not work outside the home (Bronfenbrenner and Crouter, 1982; Chase-Landsdale, Michael, and Desai, 1991; Richards and Duckett, 1991; Zaslow, Rabinovich, and Suwalsky, 1991).

As in the case of research findings on gender, findings relating to race and social class are not clearcut. While the findings of some studies indicate that the influences of mothers' employment can vary with the race and social class of the family, the findings of other studies do not support this conclusion.

We would expect the quality of the child-care arrangements available to children during their mothers' absence to be an important factor in the children's developmental progress. Indeed, there is evidence that child-care arrangements may alter the effects of maternal employment, but such arrangements seem to interact in a complex way with children's gender and family resources (Baydar and Brooks-Gunn, 1991). Much remains to be done to explicate the effects of different types of care and how such care relates to family influences and the characteristics of individual children (Thompson, 1991).

One particularly significant effect of the absence from the home of both parents during long periods is the increasing number of "self-care" children: children who have to look after themselves much of the time. It has been estimated that in the United States at least two million children of school age have no adult supervision at all after school (Hodgkinson, 1991). Sometimes, such children may have to care for younger brothers and sisters as well.

It is doubtful that children under the age of eight or nine years, in Western society at any rate, are sufficiently mature, cognitively or socially, to cope with long periods of self-care. As far as older children and adolescents are concerned, definite risks seem to be associated with self-care. For example, adolescents in this situation have been found to be more likely to become involved in substance abuse, particularly if they spend their time unsupervised at friends' homes, than are comparable adolescents who are not caring for themselves (Galambos and Maggs, 1991).

In many countries, educational programs are being established to help deal with the problems of self-care children and adolescents. These programs are aimed at teaching children how to deal with their responsibilities more effectively, responsibilities that, in many cases, include earning an income as well as caring for siblings.

One-Parent Families

Factors such as the increasing participation of women in the labor force, the instability of marriages, and personal choices of life-style have resulted in an increase in the number of one-parent families — that is, families with one or more children but only one parent, usually the mother. While belonging to such a family is sometimes only a transitory situation, the experience can no longer be considered rare. In Japan, for example, while in 1960 only 4.7 percent of households were one-parent families, twenty-five years later, 15.8 percent were of this type (Martin and Culter, 1983). In the United States, about 20 percent of all families can be classified as one-parent households. In these families, the majority of children live with the mother (U.S. Bureau of the Census, 1987). Projections indicate that the number of children who will be living in families in which one parent is not present will increase in the United States from 16.2 million (in 1984) to 21.1 million in 2020, an increase of 30 percent (Pallas, Natriello, and McDill, 1989).

The most common reason for children living with one parent is that their parents have divorced. It has been estimated that half of all marriages contracted in the United States in the mid-1970s will end in divorce (Cherlin, 1981). Despite the pervasiveness of family dissolution, relatively little is known of its long-term effects on children or parents. Several studies report that, compared to children in intact families, children in divorced families exhibit lower levels of cognitive performance and self-esteem and higher levels of delinquency, at least in the short term. However, the differences tend to be small and frequently disappear when confounding and mediating variables, such as maternal employment and family processes, are taken into account (Barber and Eccles, 1992).

Research findings on other one-parent families — that is, ones in which the parents were never married — indicate that the consequences for these children may be more negative than in the case of divorce. Many research studies provide evidence of lower scholastic achievement, earlier dropout, more absences from school, greater emotional instability, and a higher incidence of discipline and health problems among children from one-parent families than among children from two-parent families. However, it is difficult to distinguish the effects of living in a one-parent family from the effects of a variety of conditions that often are associated with such families, such as low income, family dysfunction, and poor quality of child-care arrangements (see Gouke and Rollins, 1990).

Of special concern is the issue of the adolescent mother who is often the parent in a one-parent family. The rate of births to adolescent mothers seems to be higher in the United States than in most other nations (Alan Guttmacher Institute, 1981), and the problem is clearly growing — if not in absolute numbers, at least in the recognition of the situation as problematic for both mother and child. The physical consequences of early pregnancy are frequently detrimental to both. Further, adolescent mothers tend to have low educational attainment; when married, they tend to suffer high rates of marital stress, and their employment tends to be restricted to marginal economic sectors. The children, for their part, are likely to live in poverty (Scott-Jones, 1984).

In many countries, legislation to protect the rights and security of children involved in separation and divorce is emerging. What was once considered the exception — namely, that the child is a fully recognized member of the family in the eyes of the law — is now accepted as the rule in many European countries. Where this is so, it is recognized as children's fundamental right that no decision regarding their present or future status should be made without taking into account their particular circumstances and feelings (Simitis, 1985).

Blended Families

Countries with high separation and divorce rates also tend to have high remarriage rates. In the Caribbean, for instance, where one finds very high dissolution rates within the first five years of marriage (74 percent in Haiti and 48 percent in Jamaica), women tend to remarry very soon. In Haiti, 95 percent of women involved in early dissolutions are likely to be married within the subsequent five years; the figure is 90 percent in Jamaica. On the other hand, compared to other regions of the developing world, low remarriage rates are found in Asia, particularly in Korea (43 percent) and the Philippines (46 percent) (Smith, Carrasco, and McDonald, 1984).

In the Western world, remarriage is common. It has been reported that ten years ago in the United States about 80 percent of divorced parents had remarried and 40 percent of them had divorced again (Joseph, 1986).

Remarriage can have immediate effects on children who have to adjust to perhaps quite different family circumstances, living either beween two households or with stepparents, as well as having to cope with any number of emotional and financial strains. For such children, the additional demands of school can easily prove unmanageable. With the obvious stress on the internal dynamics of the family during periods of transformation, relationships between school and parent are likely to be similarly at risk.

Families Whose Culture Differs from the Mainstream Culture

International migration patterns and the extension of school services to more and more communities are often associated with situations in which the culture of the family is significantly different from that of the mainstream school. These situations and the discontinuities between home and school that can arise from them were discussed in Chapter Two.

Current population trends indicate that family migration will continue to be a characteristic of modern societies. The numbers (and proportions) of children who live in a nonmainstream culture will continue to grow in the United States over the next three decades. For example, the number of children up to seventeen years old who spoke a language other than English as their primary language was estimated at under two million in 1982. This number is expected to triple to almost six million by the year 2020. This means that the percentage of children and youth in the United States who speak a primary language other than English will rise over this period from about 2.5 to about 7.5 (Pallas, Natriello, and McDill, 1989). For many such children, their language difficulties will place them at risk in the American educational system.

An interesting aspect of research on families from nonmainstream cultures has concerned itself with the school performance of children from Asian backgrounds. While Hispanic and black children, on average, tend to perform less well than children from the mainstream culture in the U.S. educational system, there is considerable evidence that Asian children perform better. Thus, compared to other ethnic groups, including whites, Asian Americans receive superior high school grades and higher scores on the mathematics subtest of the Scholastic Aptitude Test. They are also overrepresented in higher education (Sue and Okazaki, 1990). In their homeland, Japanese students have consistently performed extremely well in international studies of achievement.

In an effort to find the reason for the superior educational performance of Asian students, research has been carried out both in the United States and in their countries of origin. The research is of particular interest since it might provide clues to students' high achievement rather than, as is so often the case in research, to the difficulties children encounter in learning.

Several commentators have looked to the cultural values of Asians in their search for the antecedents of high scholastic achievement. One might expect that socialization and institutional practices in a culture, such as hard work, respect for education, and the motivation to become educated, might foster academic achievement. However, although ethnic differences in parenting style have been found to exist between Asians (both in the United States and in their home countries) and other cultural groups in the United States (see Hess and Azuma, 1991; Ritter and Dornbusch, 1989; Siu, 1992), these differences do not seem to account for observed ethnic differences in achievement (Sue and Okazaki, 1990).

An interesting observation on the school-related behavior of Asian Americans, from the point of view of parent involvement in their children's education, is that Chinese-American parents, particularly recent immigrants, show great respect for teachers but tend to maintain a distance from the school. The fact that their children still do well at school calls into question many common assumptions about parents' involvement. It seems that parents can care deeply about their children's education and can encourage and monitor their children's progress while not being involved in the school as volunteer or policy maker. Siu (1992) concludes from this observation that "school personnel would do well not to assume that all parents defined by the school as inactive are non-caring parents" (p. 33). Perhaps of even greater importance from the point of view of parent involvement is the challenge to schools and teachers that arises from this situation "to forge a meaningful partnership with parents from diverse cultures by creating a variety of roles and redefining parent involvement to include involvement at home" (p. 33).

The Combination of Problematic Circumstances

The conditions we have just described — working-parent families, one-parent families, blended families, and families from nonmainstream cultures — often work in combination among themselves to undermine children's formal education. Thus, children who speak a primary language other than English in the United States may also live in poverty, which is often associated with a lack of resources in the family, the school, and the community to support children's school learning. Children being raised by single mothers will have about one-third as much to spend on their needs as children in two-parent families. Further, the mothers are likely to have been poorly educated, another factor associated with children's poor school achievement and early dropout (Hodgkinson, 1991).

How problems become compounded for parents and children can be seen in the not untypical case of a single mother with a low income who is raising a child (Hodgkinson, 1991). The mother will have to pay a higher percentage of her income for housing than any other category of worker. But for that money, the accommodation she will get is unlikely to have a quiet place for the child to study. The mother will have to get to work, if she is lucky enough to have work. If her child has not commenced school, she will have to get him or her to a daycare facility, and this may involve several bus trips, both before and after work. She can only hope and pray that sickness does not interfere with her schedule and income.

It has been estimated that at least one-third of preschool children in the United States are at risk of school failure even before they enter kindergarten because of poverty, neglect, sickness, and lack of adult protection and nurturance (Hodgkinson, 1991). Further, unless there are fundamental shifts in how institutions educate their children, the number of such children can be expected to increase substantially (Pallas, Natriello, and McDill, 1989).

Conclusion

In recent decades, the family has undergone profound changes, as social evolution and economic restructuring proceeded relentlessly throughout the world. Today, the pace of change in family structure and functions is greater than it has ever been. Changes in families are making it very difficult for many of them to cope with the educational needs of their children. At the same time, the magnitude of the changes, and the concern that is frequently expressed about them, should not lead us to conclude that families are not capable of adaptation or that they cannot, whatever their form, have a positive influence on their communities and on the process of child development. Although often thought of as passive, dependent institutions, families contribute to the construction of social reality and to the future social order (Boulding, 1983). Further, despite the problems they may have, families and children often show remarkable resilience. There are many examples of single-parent families or families in which both parents work that also raise healthy and academically successful children (Oakes and Lipton, 1990). However, there are also many families who may require assistance from other agencies, including the school, if they are to meet basic needs or improve the conditions required to support their children's learning.

Although changes in society and in families have important implications for children's education in general and for the educational role of the family in particular, and although our knowledge of homes and schools is growing, our understanding of the home-school interface in relation to children's learning is still limited. However, research is opening new paths in the exploration of those relationships and to the application of its findings. We may hope that these developments will help homes, schools, and other institutions work more effectively together to provide better conditions for human development. Already, as we saw in Chapter Two, many schools and school systems recognize the need to involve parents in their work and are providing structures to do this.

SIX ◘ Programs to Promote Children's Learning

In Chapters Three and Four, we saw that studies have repeatedly demonstrated strong, positive relationships between home background and measures of children's cognitive abilities and scholastic performance. Given the power of home factors in predicting children's achievements, a question that inevitably arises for educators, parents, and policy makers is: can strategies be developed that will help parents improve the home learning environment of their children, and, if so, will such efforts positively affect children's school and cognitive achievements? In this chapter, we describe some of the efforts that have been made over the past three decades to "intervene" or effect changes in the home learning environment, with the explicit aim of improving children's cognitive abilities, readiness for school, or school learning. In Chapter Seven, we will discuss the effects of these programs.

Defining Home Intervention

Most broadly defined, home intervention is a term used to describe any program that sets out to help a family foster children's mental and/or physical development. The program can include any "direct and indirect efforts aimed at altering the course of the family's anticipated growth, development, and function" (Sigel and Laosa, 1983, pp. xi–xii). To narrow the scope,

84

we exclude "therapeutic" approaches that address family pathologies (for example, psychological counseling, treatment programs for drug abuse or family violence). As far as possible, we also exclude programs that are directed primarily at parents of children who have specific physical, emotional, or psychological needs (for example, children with physically or mentally handicapping conditions), or programs for parents whose children participate in educational programs distinct from "regular" classroom instruction (for example, special education, programs for "gifted" students, bilingual education).

With these exclusions, there still exists an enormous and varied literature on programs designed to help parents provide a more stimulating and enriched environment for children's cognitive growth (primarily in the preschool years) and/or teach and reinforce the concepts, skills, and attitudes expected and required in school (mostly for preschool or school-aged children). Some of the programs are broad based. For example, *family support programs* usually include components of nutrition, health care, and social services, in addition to those directed at the intellectual and school-related environment of the home. These programs recognize that for many families the first step toward improving home conditions for children's cognitive development is to meet the family's basic physical, economic, and social needs.

More narrow in scope than family support programs are *parent education programs,* which concentrate on the role of parents as partners in their children's education and attempt to alter some aspect of parental knowledge, attitudes, or behaviors, with a view to improving children's cognitive and school performance. Such programs differ from *parent education* or *parenthood education,* which is designed to help parents or prospective parents learn about child rearing and child development principles. They also differ from *parent involvement* and *parent participation* programs, which tend to be directed by the school and attempt to involve parents in school activities and/or teach parents specific skills and strategies for teaching or reinforcing school tasks at home.

These terms represent clear conceptual distinctions. In practice, it is often difficult to clearly categorize any one individual program. Program designers draw methods and strategies from their own experiences, other programs, research literature, and the needs and desires of local sponsors and participants, with the result that their methods and strategies cut across conceptual boundaries. Nevertheless, in the following sections we will try to define some of the trends in philosophies and methods within the broad spectrum of home intervention over the last twenty to thirty years, describe programs that illustrate different philosophies or approaches, and conclude by highlighting some issues that guide current parent education efforts.

Trends in Home Intervention Programs

Any discussion of contemporary trends in home intervention must begin by acknowledging that formal efforts to teach parents how to teach their children have a long history. Some authors begin such histories in the seventeenth century, with the teachings of Comenius and the competing doctrines of Calvin (see, for example, Florin and Dokecki, 1983), both of whom articulated active roles for parents in directing early learning experiences with a view to shaping children's behaviors and accomplishments. Shifts in goals, methods, and types of intervention from the 1800s through the first half of this century have been well documented in comprehensive reviews (see Clarke-Stewart and Apfel, 1978; Fine, 1980; Florin and Dokecki, 1983; Schlossman, 1976). Here, we will focus on more recent history, drawing upon these reviews and adding data and perspectives published more recently. In general, there has been a movement (at least in theory) from the "deficit model" underlying the home intervention programs of the 1960s, to a "difference model" for parent education in the 1970s and early 1980s, to the current emphasis on "empowerment models" for parent and family education.

The Deficit Model

During the 1960s, the compensatory education movement in the United States spawned a massive effort at early intervention to break the "cycle of poverty" experienced by children from low-income families. As we saw in Chapter Two, on beginning school, children from such backgrounds often lack the school readiness skills possessed by children from middle-income homes, and the gap in achievement widens with each additional year of schooling. Without successful experiences in school, students are unable to take advantage of further educational opportunities and the accompanying economic and social rewards. It was reasoned that the initial disadvantages suffered by such children must result from the lack of opportunity during the preschool years to develop school-related skills at home. The years between birth and age six were regarded as "critical periods," in which the rapid development of important intellectual functions determined the course of future cognitive growth and achievement (Bloom, 1964). Since the evidence seemed to indicate that deficiencies in these early years were not being countered effectively by subsequent school experiences, the home environment became a natural target of efforts to equalize economic and educational opportunities.

Efforts to intervene during the early years of children's development first took the form of center-based programs such as Head Start. These programs provided supplemental educational experiences, most often in special centers or a school setting, for a few hours a day, a few months a year. Among the scores of early childhood programs established during this period, many included home- or parent-based components, designed to teach parents specific behaviors that would facilitate the cognitive and social development of their children.

During this period, home intervention efforts were aimed at low-income parents of young children (infants to preschoolers). The programs were based on the explicit assumption that targeted families failed to provide the stimulation, resources, and interactions necessary to prepare their children for the tasks and demands of school. As Goodson and Hess (1976) stated in their often-cited review of twenty-eight home intervention programs of the 1960s: "The first [assumption of these programs], which we call the home deficit assumption, is that the home in a low income community often is an environment that fails to prepare the young child adequately for successful entry in the first grades of public school. This assumption is based on research showing that lower-class or lower-income homes are different from middle-class homes on a number of variables presumably significant in a child's development, such as type and pattern of stimulation, language style, pattern of parent-child interactions, motivation, etc." (p. 13). Goodson and Hess defined these programs as "developed by professionals for the purpose of instructing parents in techniques for preparing their own young children in school relevant skills" (p. 5). In choosing the behaviors and skills that parents were to be taught, "these programs involve[d] an implicit standard of parenting that is considered most likely to produce intelligent, well-adjusted, academically successful children" (p. 2).

Early evaluations indicated that children in Head Start and similar programs made substantial initial gains in cognitive performance and school readiness skills. Those who participated in programs with a parent- or home-based component sustained these gains three to four years after the program had ended (Bronfenbrenner, 1974; Goodson and Hess, 1976). Such reports (see also Bauch, Vietze, and Morris, 1973) solidified the popular consensus that involving and educating parents should be an integral part of early childhood intervention (Florin and Dokecki, 1983).

While the deficit approach is still prevalent in many programs aimed at low-income or minority families and their children, observers have long noted that the model has several deficiencies of its own. First, the deficit view of disadvantaged backgrounds was based on findings that children from such backgrounds performed poorly on conventional ability and achievement tests in schools and that their use of language seemed to be less well developed than that of children from more privileged backgrounds. Further, these poorer levels of performance were often attributed to a lack of opportunities in the home to develop a range of intellectual and language skills. However, the research findings relating to deficit were not unequivocal (Goodson and Hess, 1976). For example, some research pointed to the dangers of overgeneralizing about the skills and potential of disadvantaged children on the basis of their poorer performance on school tasks. When such children were observed functioning in settings more relaxed and informal than school, they were found to exhibit a level of language use that was complex, elaborate, and internally consistent for a range of cognitive and social purposes (Houston, 1970; Labov, 1972). Further, while their poorer performance on scholastic ability tests might reflect a lack of opportunity to acquire certain knowledge and skills, it should not be taken as an index of their inability to learn (Rohwer, 1971).

A second basis for criticizing early intervention efforts was that they often worked on the assumption that any program model could work with any parents (Powell, 1988). A problem with this position is that even if children from disadvantaged backgrounds share difficulties in adapting to the work of school, the nature of the disadvantage may vary greatly from child to child. In some homes, children may actually suffer a nutritional deficit that impedes their ability to learn at school (Pollitt, 1990). In other cases (as we saw in Chapter Two), the child's difficulty might arise because he or she comes from a particular ethnic background or from a family that follows a particular life-style sufficiently different from the school's environment to cause problems. Obviously, a wide variety of life-styles exist, not only from country to country but from one ethnic group to another within the same country or from one family to another within the same community. Such differences in background have implications for a program of parent involvement. Only when the needs and characteristics of families have been assessed is it possible to specify the program that is likely to be most beneficial.

A third criticism of early intervention efforts arises from the fact that, with a few exceptions, the social context in which families functioned received little attention in program design (Powell, 1988). However, it is now recognized that since such contexts may be crucial for the functioning of families, a program that does not take account of their role is less likely to be successful than one that does. The importance of the social context of families is most clearly recognized in views that locate the origins of the problems of disadvantage precisely in those social contexts. Powell (1988) states this position succinctly when he says that "failures in the social environment, and not personal deficiencies, are the cause of deprivation or suffering" (p. 15). The failures are perceived to be particularly evident in the way power and wealth are distributed in society; when people lack power and wealth, disadvantage is likely to arise.

Fourth, the model assumed that the school environment, with its norms and standards of behavior, is superior to that of families who live "out of the mainstream." Finally, the approach increased already-existing pressures on targeted families, implying that, in addition to coping with the problems of poverty and assimilation into the dominant culture, parents should be providing more for their children (an approach often dubbed "blaming the victim").

Even as deficit approaches were being implemented, assumptions and approaches were changing. Thus, some program sponsors preferred to consider themselves "facilitators" rather than "interveners." Their approach involved attempting to help parents identify their own goals and then plan and implement appropriate educational programs with their children. The educational interchange between parents and professionals was moving toward "a sharing process, away from didactic intervention" (Goodson and Hess, 1976, p. 14).

The Difference Model

In the 1970s, the home intervention programs born of the compensatory education movement evolved into a new generation of programs. Like the earlier programs, these focused on low-income families and had the same goal of "boosting" underprivileged children's cognitive, social, and academic attainments. But program sponsors espoused a different philosophy and set of assumptions. For example, Florin and Dokecki (1983) describe the Parent-Child Development Centers (formed in 1969) as being based on a "cultural difference model," which is closely related to the home-school discontinuity approach described in Chapter Two. The approach recognized the strengths, experience, and knowledge of parents; individual programs were planned and implemented for each site, recognizing the importance of adapting an educational intervention to community needs and characteristics. Programs sought to provide a broad range of services that would prepare parents to rear their children and to negotiate transactions with societal institutions. Further, the form of delivery shifted from didactic instruction by an expert to a more active collaboration between parent and parent educator in determining and meeting parents' needs.

In this approach, the school environment and culture is not viewed as inherently superior; rather, differences between the cultures of home and school are recognized, and attempts are made to help the child adjust to a "different" environment in the school. Theoretically, the approach recognizes different styles of thinking, with accompanying patterns of strengths and weaknesses, which are viewed as "stylistic" patterns rather than as differences in cognitive capacity. Zigler and Berman (1983) explained: "The difference model surely provides a more realistic view of group and individual differences in behavior. It also encourages a more productive approach to intervention in which we do not try to change children but instead try to build on the strengths that they bring to the program. In adopting a difference rather than a deficit model, optimal development is no longer sought by inculcating middle-class values but by discovering ways to allow various intellectual and personal potentials to emerge in other than middle-class settings" (p. 895).

"Cultural appropriateness" continues to be a central concern of many educational enhancement or educational intervention programs, as well as of programs that seek to recognize and build upon the family's own culture and traditions to provide learning experiences in the home that will reinforce school-based concepts and skills. As one example, Family Math materials and activities have been adapted for American Indians to show parents how to emphasize math skills in their teaching of tribal customs and skills, such as beading; similar adaptations are evident in the translations of materials for families of Hispanic and Chinese backgrounds. Myers (1988) describes programs in Asia, Africa, Latin America, and the Middle East that appear to incorporate locally developed, culturally appropriate materials, or to adapt existing programs for the target culture (for example, the Turkish adaptation of HIPPY, the Home Intervention Program for Preschool Youngsters).

Rather than carrying with it a well-defined set of programs, however, the difference model seems to have served as a bridge between the home intervention programs based on the deficit model and emergent "parent and family education" programs that aim to "empower" parents to assume and perform their various roles more effectively.

The Empowerment Model

It was partly in response to criticisms of earlier intervention approaches and the fact that a deficit view of children and families might have demoralizing effects on participants that more recent programs introduced the concepts of partnership and empowerment. These concepts have been interpreted in a variety of ways. The concept of partnership means that parties should work together. It recognizes that the parent is the child's principal educator and that the roles of parent and teacher (or program staff) are equal and complementary, sharing the same purpose and characterized by mutual respect, information sharing, and decision making (Bastiani, 1989; Pugh and De'Ath, 1989). In this view, the professional's role is best viewed as that of facilitator in achieving goals and carrying out activities that have been determined jointly by both parties (Powell, 1988). Indeed, parents can be seen as consumers of child development information and, as such, should be offered a choice of options from which to choose.

Partnership is not confined to the relationship between parent and teacher or between parent and program staff but may be extended to other relevant parties. As already mentioned, earlier programs were criticized for taking little account of the broader social context in which families operate. The idea of partnership meets this criticism on two grounds. First, it recognizes that the problems of disadvantage very often have their origins in the conditions of the families' communities, which may lack services, organization, leadership, or indeed any sense of being able to deal with their many problems. In such situations, the development of the community may be seen as a prerequisite to sustaining the effects of any intervention to support children's development. This can be a slow, difficult, and sensitive task, especially if proposals for improvement are to originate in the community rather than from outside.

The idea of partnership also recognizes that individuals and families are members of multiple environments and that "nested connections" exist between individuals, families, and larger groups and organizations (Bronfenbrenner, 1986). Since many agencies besides the family play a role in supporting child development, partnership with a variety of formal and informal social systems and organizations may be necessary to obtain optimal conditions for children's development. It is for this reason that many parent involvement programs seek to promote the development of partnerships between informal social systems made up of family members, friends, neighbors, and coworkers, as well as with more distant but also influential economic and cultural institutions, such as the school, the workplace, church, and public services (Cochran, 1988).

A partnership strategy is often linked to the concept of empowerment of individuals. Approaches based on this idea are designed first to allow parents to play a key role in their children's development, and second, in the longer term, to take more control of their own lives, so that they can influence public policy and programs and can participate effectively in economic activity (Rappaport, 1981). Empowerment programs acknowledge the strengths of families, work with parents as equal partners in assessing needs and implementing programs, recognize the family's position in and interactions with the broader socioecological context, and strive to mobilize resources relevant to promoting growth and learning in both the home and school (Myers, 1988).

The empowerment approach, in which the concepts of power and control are central, is based on the idea that people's circumstances can be changed by people themselves. It aims to help parents gain control over their own lives, to become more effective advocates for themselves and for their children in interacting with social agencies and institutions, and to engage more actively in the education of their children, by direct involvement or by obtaining resources.

Not only do proponents of empowerment believe that people can change their circumstances, they believe that the changes are likely to be more beneficial and lasting when they are effected by those in need of change rather than by outsiders. However, to reach this point, it may be necessary for outsiders to facilitate the process by affirming and reinforcing people's belief in themselves and by providing opportunities for individuals to develop their abilities to manage their own affairs. This should all be done in an atmosphere of respect for people's ways of doing things (Paz, 1990).

One of the better-known empowerment programs is the Family Matters Project (Cochran and Dean, 1991; Cochran and Woolever, 1983), which is based on five beliefs. First, all families have strengths and these, rather than deficits, should be emphasized. Second, useful knowledge about child rearing resides in parents, communities, and social networks, not just in experts. Third, different family forms are legitimate and can promote healthy children and healthy adults. Fourth, fathers should be integrally involved. And fifth, cultural differences are both valid and valuable (Cochran and Woolever, 1983).

This philosophy is reflected in the program in several ways. To begin with, eligibility for participation is not limited to any one ethnic group or socioeconomic class. In addition, the project uses an array of techniques to promote parents' self-confidence and self-esteem, to reinforce and encourage parent-child interactions, to share information about social services and institutional procedures, and to facilitate the development of social networks that provide support and resources. Also, the program organizers take a "developmental perspective" by recognizing that empowerment is a process, with steps or stages through which parents progress. They define these steps as a change in the parents' perception of self, an expansion of the parents' social network, and the development of effective relationships and interactions between parents and more distant organizations (Cochran and Dean, 1991). In summarizing their approach, the authors state: "We wanted to give parents the confidence to take responsibility and action on behalf of themselves and their children by building trust through home visiting, mutual support through informal network ties, and the special skills related to having influences in the school setting" (Cochran and Dean, 1991, p. 263).

Although there is considerable overlap between programs representing these different models, individual programs often have distinct philosophies, assumptions, and approaches. The programs also represent an evolution in the recognition and acceptance of the complexities of parents' roles and family relationships in any culture, an appreciation of the challenges faced by modern families in industrialized nations, and a recognition of the importance of assessing the existing needs of target families and of adapting programs to fit the families' needs in the context of local communities and the larger society or culture.

Types of Home Intervention Programs

We turn now from conceptual issues regarding assumptions and philosophies to a more practical discussion of different types of home intervention programs. We will consider two broad categories: comprehensive, or "family support," programs that provide a range of services and experiences and more "traditional" programs designed to teach parents specific techniques for interacting with children or providing learning opportunities outside of school.

Comprehensive Programs

Comprehensive programs provide a range of services for families and children. Nutrition (meals, counseling), health care (check-ups, screenings, immunizations, referrals), social service referrals, instruction in child-rearing practices, educational materials to use at home, peer support groups — all these, in various combinations, may be included in a comprehensive program. The programs referred to in the preceding section (for example, Parent-Child Development Centers, the Family Matters Project) represent examples of comprehensive family support programs in the United States. A comprehensive approach is considered particularly important in the developing countries, where there may be a need to provide nutritional and medical services to counter the debilitating health and developmental effects of poverty.

Two recent reviews describe projects and studies throughout Latin America, Africa, the Middle East, and Asia that take an integrated and comprehensive approach to early intervention (Halpern and Myers, 1985; Myers, 1988). Many programs place nutrition and health care first, supplemented by preschool education for children and instruction or support for mothers. Two examples cited by Myers (1988) illustrate this approach. The Integrated Child Development Services (ICDS) program in India "was designed to render supplementary nutrition, immunization, health check-ups, health and nutritional education, and non-formal pre-school education to children under 6 years and [education] to women of childbearing years . . . . The service now reaches several millions of children and mothers, mainly through *anganwadi* centers (literally, courtyards)" (p. 11), where paraprofessionals are assisted by a helper and supported by an ICDS worker. The second example Myers describes is Project PROMESA in Colombia, which includes a program to help mothers foster intellectual development in children aged three to seven through daily interactions and games; building and community service projects to improve the quality of the local water supply and to dispose of garbage and waste; education and vocational training for adults to improve income-generating skills; an early stimulation program for mothers of children up to three years of age; and nutrition programs to provide food to preschoolers and nutrition education to mothers.

Current programs in the United States include the Head Start Transition Demonstration projects, funded in 1991. Over twenty-five sites across the country are charged with designing local collaborative programs (between Head Start centers and local educational agencies) to provide transition services, family support services, and health care screenings and referrals to Head Start children and their families through the third grade. Entering their first implementation year, these programs will be evaluated locally and nationally to discern the long-term effects of providing continued comprehensive services and programs to this population of children and families.

Traditional Parent Education Programs

Traditional parent education programs tend to focus on a specific set of parent behaviors (or a specific content area) by teaching parents techniques and strategies for reinforcing their children's cognitive or scholastic skills. Some are designed for parents of preschool children to improve children's school readiness; others are for parents of school-aged children. While low-income or less well-educated parents are often the targeted populations, theoretically the techniques are made available to any interested parent. Thousands of these programs are in operation all over the world, offered through research projects, schools, districts, educational agencies, community organizations, for-profit organizations, or individual consultants. Some have focused on verbal interactions, some on parental teaching behaviors, others on reading or other school subjects.

Verbal Interactions. In preschool programs, verbal interactions between parent and child are frequently the focus of attention. Focus may be on increasing the quantity of verbal interactions (by encouraging parents to verbalize more during play, for example) or on improving the quality of the interactions, such as increasing parents' use of more complex or elaborated language with their children (see Kessen and Fein, 1975; Levenstein, 1970). The tone or responsiveness of parents during these verbal interactions may also be emphasized (see Clarke-Stewart and Apfel, 1978; Slaughter, 1983).

Parental Teaching Behaviors. Many programs offer specific educational materials or activities for parents to use at home, or teach parents ways to interact with and instruct their children in verbal communication or problem solving. One such example is to be found in the Parent Education Follow-Through Project (Olmsted, 1991; Olmsted and Rubin, 1982). "Desirable teaching behaviors" are specified for parents to use in interactions, such as asking "higher-order questions." The programs also offer guidelines (and materials) for "home learning activities," which are designed to complement or extend classroom learning, to incorporate home materials and home activities into learning situations, and to focus on the process of learning rather than on finding correct answers.

Reading. One of the most common strategies in parent education programs is to teach parents to become better models for and facilitators of their children's reading at home. Enhancing parents' abilities to encourage and reinforce their children's reading is considered to be particularly important because of the strong relationship between out-of-school reading and children's performance in school. A number of studies have demonstrated a relationship between frequency and amount of reading outside of school and children's reading achievement (Anderson, Wilson, and Fielding, 1988; Greaney, 1980; Walberg and Tsai, 1984). Indeed, in the study by Anderson, Wilson, and Fielding, reading books was the out-of-school activity that proved to have the strongest association with reading proficiency.

Parents' roles in developing their children's reading abilities can take a variety of forms. Silvern (1985), for example, defined five categories: (1) reading to children — which increases their listening and speaking vocabularies, symbol recognition, comprehension skills, and length of spoken sentences; (2) interactive practices while reading — asking questions, encouraging children to ask questions, talking about the reading; (3) availability (not necessarily ownership) of reading materials and parents' modeling through their own reading practices, which have been found to be related to children's interest in and value of reading as well as their achievement; (4) rewards and expectations — expecting children to learn to read and encouraging their learning through praise and providing them with more reading materials; (5) guidance and instruction — assisting children in setting goals and selecting reading material, using resources, talking about what children have read, listening to them read, and instructing them in the techniques and mechanics of reading. Programs that involve parents in their children's reading may focus on any of these variables and can take various forms, from simply encouraging parents to read to or listen to their children read to more formal "contracts" defining types of activities, the amount of time to be spent, and the materials to be read.

The Haringey Project in England provides a good example of an effective program to involve parents in their children's reading (Hewison, 1988; Tizard, Shoefield, and Hewison, 1982). The program was targeted to working-class parents, who were encouraged to engage in specific reading practices with their children (aged six to eight years). Teachers sent home materials for parents to read with their children; there was a system for logging in or checking the completion of these reading materials; and program staff conducted home visits to discuss strategies that parents could use in helping their children with reading. Parents did increase reading activities at home and the improvements in their children's reading performance were quite strong. Several other programs have also reported success related to reading after involving parents in home learning activities (Becher, 1984; Hannon, 1987; MacLeod, 1985; Silvern, 1985).

Other Subjects. Recent years have seen the appearance of programs that encourage parents to become more involved in their children's mathematics or science learning. These programs may involve special classes for parents and children to take together, such as the Family Math program or "family science" classes at museums and science centers (Ostlund, Gennaro, and Dobbert, 1985), or they may involve sending materials home from school to help parents help their children with homework in these subjects (for example, the "Teachers Involve Parents in Schoolwork: TIPS" materials produced by the Center for Research on Elementary and Middle Schools at Johns Hopkins University; see also Rich, 1987). These programs have been successful in recruiting parents to attend special classes and have produced high-quality materials for parents to use at home.

Methods and Strategies for Working with Parents

The one distinguishing characteristic of home- or parent-based intervention programs is that a "parent educator" or "facilitator" works with a parent or family member to teach strategies to use with the child at home. This approach differs from the approach of school-based interventions, which attempt to enrich children's experience through supplemental school activities. It also differs from home-based tutoring programs in which a professional comes into the home to work directly with a child but does not involve the parent.

Beyond sharing the basic characteristics of working with parents, these types of home intervention programs vary considerably in their form, content, and methods. Program staff may conduct home visits to work individually with parent and child or they may work with groups of parents at a special center or at school. The mother alone may be involved or children may participate with their parents or with other family members. Program services may be delivered through formal workshops, the media, special demonstrations, materials sent to the parent at home, or any other method that parent educators might design to reach parents in the targeted group.

In keeping with the trend toward more comprehensive programs, most parent educators advocate using a variety of methods when working with parents. Olmsted (1991), for example, suggests that several alternatives should be made available to parents: involvement in schools or classrooms; group meetings of parents alone or with school staff; one-on-one meetings between parents and school staff or program facilitators; provision of materials and activities to use at home; and utilization of community resources or agencies (for example, adult education, libraries). The Child and Family Neighborhood Program offers weekly parent meetings, which are facilitated by a community-based paraprofessional and supplemented by a weekly open house and series of special events (Powell, 1983). In the Family Matters Project, attempts were initially made to have parents choose either home visits or group meetings, for research purposes. However, when the two strategies were eventually made available to all participants, overall participation increased (Cochran and Woolever, 1983). Obviously, offering a variety of options and approaches allows parents to pick the format with which they are most comfortable as well as allowing program organizers to use different formats to achieve different goals.

Few formal studies have focused on identifying the "best" methods for working with parents. Some principles do seem to emerge fairly consistently, however, from experience, common sense, or preliminary evaluation evidence. First, programs that provide structure and concrete activities seem to be more effective than ones that attempt to teach general principles of parent-child interaction. Talking with parents about specific types of interactions, or working with parents and children together, helps to link advice to parents' own experiences. Second, sustained contact and interaction with parents over a period of time helps to solidify and reinforce the concepts and principles. One-shot workshops or classes are not likely to produce results as good as a relationship developed with a parent over several months. Third, there seem to be strong advantages associated with offering opportunities for one-to-one sessions with the parent educator, in conjunction with group sessions among parents led by a facilitator. Private sessions allow the parent educator to focus on the parent's individual needs and situation and can encourage the development of trust and mutual respect. Cochran and Woolever (1983) found that some parents needed this individual contact before they would venture out to group meetings. Group meetings, on the other hand, provide the opportunity to share ideas and to develop support networks with other parents; this may be a critical factor in encouraging parents to try new strategies with their children at home. The camaraderie and mutual support of group meetings are also likely to be more enjoyable and meaningful to parents than a more didactic approach.

Conclusion

In summarizing trends in parent education philosophies, goals, and methods, we have referred to many issues that seem to be shaping current efforts and future directions in this field. One is the issue of providing comprehensive programs for families to help them meet their physical, economic, and social needs as a necessary step in enabling them to provide more stimulating and enriched environments for learning in the home. A second issue is that of recognizing family strengths and cultural contexts and drawing upon these in designing and delivering programs. The third concern is to find ways to tailor programs to fit the needs, interests, and priorities of individual families and of families from a variety of cultural or socioeconomic groups. Given the stresses of modern society, families from all walks of life may need access to resources and education to enable them to support their children's learning and development.

Future efforts should be informed by lessons learned from the study and evaluation of home intervention programs in general and parent education programs in particular over the past three decades. To the extent that these efforts have been successful, they further confirm the power and influence of parent behaviors on children's cognitive development and achievement. They also enable us to strengthen and direct that influence to improve children's learning. In the following chapter, we consider the effects of home intervention, as reported in formal research and evaluation.

The Effectiveness ▪ SEVEN
of Family Intervention
Programs

In this chapter, we draw upon reviews of studies that have examined the effects of programs designed to help parents become stronger partners in their children's education (see, for example, Bronfenbrenner, 1974; Clarke-Stewart and Apfel, 1978; Florin and Dokecki, 1983; Goodson and Hess, 1976; Halpern, 1986; Hess and Holloway, 1984; Lazar and others, 1977). We also look at the results of more recent studies that have examined the evidence of the impact of parent education and home intervention programs on parents and children. We will examine evidence on the effects of such programs on children's cognitive and school performance and on parent and home variables. Before considering this evidence, however, a number of methodological concerns should be mentioned that are relevant to interpreting the findings of studies.

First, a problem arises from the fact that the findings of individual studies or evaluations of specific programs are often difficult to compare directly with other studies or programs. This is partly because major differences between programs in their goals and methods, in the ages of the children involved, and in the characteristics of participating families make it difficult to assess, across studies, the effects of specific intervention strategies on parent or child characteristics. Second, many programs do not have formal evaluation components, or they collect only "informal" data that cannot be readily interpreted outside the context of a particular study (see Clarke-Stewart and Apfel, 1978). Third, when formal evaluations are carried out within one study or program, the variables measured and the instruments used to assess those variables may not be comparable to those of other studies or programs.

Fourth, it is extremely difficult to establish clear causal links between changes in parent variables and subsequent measures of children's performance or development. Many programs do not assess changes in parent variables at all, choosing to focus solely on measures of children's performance. Experimental studies (which would provide the strongest basis for making causal inferences), in which families are randomly assigned to "treatment" and "nontreatment" (or control) groups and relevant variables are controlled during the treatment period, are extremely difficult to implement in natural settings. Further, issues of equity and equal access may prevent researchers from withholding treatments from control-group families.

Effects on Children's Cognitive and School Performance

A major purpose of many home intervention and parent education programs is to improve children's opportunities for learning. Most program evaluations, therefore, include measures of children's cognitive and scholastic achievements as indicators of effectiveness. One of the most common child variables assessed in evaluations of home intervention programs (particularly those for infants, toddlers, and preschoolers) has been general intelligence. Measures of general intelligence are moderately strong predictors of school performance, are readily available, and have well-documented psychometric properties. However, concerns about the cultural biases of such measures and about their appropriateness in assessing programs in which the goals are to improve school achievement or social functioning have led to the use of a broader array of instruments that measure a variety of child variables. Thus, evaluations have included various direct and indirect measures of school performance, such as scores on standardized achievement tests, school grades, teacher ratings, and student self-reports. Some studies have included attitudinal and socioemotional variables and assessments of more comprehensive outcomes, such as "social competence," that might include physical health, formal cognition, achievement, and motivational and emotional variables (see Zigler and Trickett, 1978).

As with many child-centered interventions, programs that include a parent component have been found to result in gains in children's cognitive achievements. In a comprehensive review of preschool parent training programs, Clarke-Stewart and Apfel (1978) concluded that working with mothers to improve the quality of intellectual stimulation and verbal interaction in the home has immediate effects on children's intellectual performance and development. Most of the studies reviewed reported significant or at least moderate gains in the intelligence quotient (IQ) of children in home intervention programs, compared to children of nonparticipating parents. Some studies also showed gains in language and verbal ability. In another review, of twenty-eight preschool home intervention programs for disadvantaged children, Goodson and Hess (1976) also found evidence of immediate and positive gains in IQ scores for children whose parents had participated. Significant, positive relationships have also been found between parents' participation in preschool programs and children's performance on specific assessments of reasoning ability, school-related knowledge and skills, and verbal concepts (see, for example, Irvine, 1979).

Other studies have documented improvements in children's school performance. In a meta-analysis of twenty-nine controlled studies of school-based family intervention programs for children from kindergarten through twelfth grade, the programs were found to have had considerable effects on children's school learning (Graue, Weinstein, and Walberg, 1983). The median effect size of .50 that was found indicates that the typical program raised the performance of students in the intervention group from the fiftieth to the sixty-ninth percentile of the control-group distribution. Effects appeared to be stronger when teachers received special training and when special facilities were provided for the program. Another review of studies from the 1970s also found that children whose parents participated in parent education programs demonstrated significant gains in achievement test scores and other indicators of school success (Florin and Dokecki, 1983).

Upon reviewing programs for parents of elementary school children, A. T. Henderson (1981, 1984) concluded that school-directed efforts to improve family support for children's school learning produced significant, long-lasting effects. When parents were taught how to take more active roles in monitoring, reinforcing, guiding, and facilitating their children's out-of-school learning time, their children performed better in school. Comprehensive, sustained programs to teach parents to reinforce school learning at home have been found to result in notable improvements in a range of student characteristics — achievement levels, achievement motivation, attitudes toward schooling, and school attendance (see Becher, 1984; Comer, 1984, 1988; Epstein, 1987a; Janhom, 1983; Moles, 1982; Rich, 1985, 1987; Sattes, 1985).

Given the importance of reading skills for nearly all school subjects, reading achievement is a commonly used criterion for assessing the effectiveness of intervention programs for school-aged children. It has been found that teaching parents to encourage and reinforce reading at home can produce dramatic improvements in their children's reading skills and attitudes toward reading. Encouraging parents to read to their children more often, to listen to them read, or to help them with the mechanics of reading has been shown to significantly increase children's performance on a wide range of reading tasks and tests (see reviews by Becher, 1984; Silvern, 1985; also Hewison, 1988; Tizard, Shoefield, and Hewison, 1982; Toomey, 1986).

The effects of involving parents in reading seem to be strongest for younger children. For example, in a Title I parent education program involving over eight hundred children in first through sixth grades, a 20 percent increase was found in the number of first graders reading at grade level after one year; however, the percentage declined steadily across grade levels, until at sixth grade, the increase was only 5.5 percent (Gross, 1974). There also was evidence that children who were reading poorly at the beginning of a program benefited more from increased parent involvement than children whose performance was at or above average from the start. This may have been because parents of "good" readers were already encouraging reading at home (Hewison, 1988; Irvine, 1979).

Gains in mathematics achievement have been less frequently reported in research. Evidence of such gains, however, is to be found in some studies aimed at teaching parents to increase the "cognitive level" of interactions with their children (Olmsted and Rubin, 1982) or to provide more intellectual stimulation in the home (Guinagh and Gordon, 1976). Some programs aimed at improving the level of academic support and guidance for school learning in the home have demonstrated notable improvements in children's scores on standardized tests in mathematics (Janhom, 1983), but others have not (Epstein, 1991a). Since few studies have assessed children's mathematics achievement, there is relatively little evidence of the effects of home intervention on that aspect of students' school performance.

Positive results from teaching parents to support school learning have been demonstrated across different cultures. For example, Janhom (1983) implemented a home intervention program based on the principles presented in Chapter Nine of this book with 218 parents of fourth-grade children in Chiang Mai, Thailand, and found that children's school achievements increased dramatically over a six-month period. For the study, parents of children in eight classes were randomly assigned to one of three treatment groups or to a control group. In the treatment groups, parents learned about materials, activities, and strategies to use at home to support and reinforce their children's school learning. They also received specific information regarding textbooks, schoolwork, and child-rearing principles. Standardized tests of language (vocabulary, reading comprehension, language usage, and spelling) and of mathematics (basic skills, problem solving) were administered to the children before and after the intervention.

At the end of the six months, children from the three treatment groups demonstrated significant gains in achievement test scores compared to the children of nonparticipating parents (the control group). Students whose parents demonstrated the greatest increase in support of their children's learning gained as much as 4 standard deviation units in achievement compared to nontreatment children. Gains for other students were lower (1.5 to 2.5 standard deviation units) but were still significant compared to the average performance of the control-group children.

In another study carried out in Southeast Asia, a remedial-support program was provided for the parents of second-grade children from poor homes in Malaysia. The program, which ran for about seven months, consisted of teacher-parent workshops in which parents were taught how to produce and use supportive reading materials for home and school. At the end of the program, the mean level of the children's reading achievement had increased by about 1 standard deviation unit. Two factors were found to be related to improvement: the degree of the parents' involvement in the program (as indicated by attendance at workshops and production of materials) and the quality of the parents' feedback for their children's reading (consisting of the parents' approval of their children's responses and their toleration of incorrect responses) (Atan, Haji Abdullah, Bakar Nordin, and Remot, 1982). In reviews of comprehensive family support and preschool education programs throughout Latin America, significant gains in measures of children's cognitive development, school achievement, and school retention rates have also been reported (Halpern and Myers, 1985; Myers, 1988).

There is evidence that the effects of home intervention programs during the preschool years can persist for several years. Some longitudinal studies have demonstrated that IQ effects of programs that include a parent component are maintained into the elementary school years (Goodson and Hess, 1976; Kellaghan, 1977b; Lazar and others, 1977). Although there is a consistent tendency for IQ gains to "fade" after two or three years, the initial gains may be important in increasing children's school readiness and early school performance during the "foundation-building" years and in decreasing the risk of special education placements during the primary grades—factors that, in turn, may contribute to subsequent achievement and school success.

Long-term gains in school achievement have been documented in a variety of programs. In a follow-up study of a group of ninety-one children whose parents had participated in preschool intervention programs, Guinagh and Gordon (1976) found that, six years after program participation, the children had significantly higher scores on reading and mathematics tests than did their nonparticipating peers and that fewer were assigned to special education or remedial classes (5 percent compared to 25 percent in the control group). In a longitudinal study of Project HOPE (Home-Oriented Preschool Education), children aged three to five, whose parents were taught to reinforce and augment daily lessons broadcast on television, still demonstrated higher levels of achievement (grade-point averages and basic-skills test scores) five to seven years following the program than did children who only viewed the TV lessons (Gotts, 1980). Other researchers have reported similar differences between children whose parents had been involved in programs and children whose parents had not on the children's achievement test scores, grade-retention rates, and special education placements, two to four years following program participation (for example, Gray and Klaus, 1970; Lazar and others, 1977; Palmer, 1977; Sprigle, 1974).

Several of the studies we have just considered compared the performance of children who had participated in a home intervention program with the performance of children who had not. Another approach compares the performance of children who participated in a program that had a home-based component with the performance of children who participated in a school-based program only. In one such study, Radin (1969) compared the reading readiness levels of high-IQ children who had been enrolled in one of three groups in an experimental kindergarten program. Children in Group 1 attended a half-day kindergarten in addition to a half-day of supplemental classes; they also received biweekly visits from a home counselor. Parents were shown how to use home teaching materials and how to reinforce what was being taught in the classroom. Children in other groups attended classes but did not have the home visits. Although children in all groups made significant gains in reading readiness, those showing the greatest growth (in reading as well as on the Stanford-Binet Intelligence Scale) were the children in Group 1. A study with low-IQ children in a preschool program produced similar results. Further, children from the parent involvement group showed continued growth in verbal ability at the end of their kindergarten year (Radin, 1972).

In another study of over two thousand disadvantaged children in grades 2 through 6, students whose parents were trained in methods of reinforcing reading performance at home (through "performance contracts") scored significantly higher on standardized tests of reading achievement than did children of nonparticipating parents (Gillum, 1977). Similar findings have been reported by Hewison (1988) for a special reading program involving parents of low socioeconomic status in England. Compared to other groups of students who received only "extra help from the teacher," the children in the home-based group showed significant short- and long-term gains in reading performance. Further, the proportion of "weak readers" in the parent involvement group was reduced, compared to both local and national norms.

It should be noted that not all studies have demonstrated increased short-term benefits (as measured by child outcomes) of a parent- or home-based program, compared to a program that focuses solely on the child. The Head Start Delivery Modes project compared the effects of center-based, home-based, and mixed-model delivery modes on parents' and children's literacy (Peters, Bollin, and Murphy, 1991). Children in all groups made significant gains in IQ and in language, reading, mathematics, and science (as measured by the Head Start Measures Battery). Children in the groups with a parent component performed at about the same level on the posttests as did those who had participated in the center-based program. Home Start programs, in which the Head Start curriculum and philosophies were conveyed through the home with minimal direct staff involvement with the child, demonstrated gains in children's school readiness (Love and others, 1976). However, Home Start children often performed at a comparable level to children who had participated in the Head Start (center-based) programs. In a recent reanalysis of previous reviews, White, Taylor, and Moss (1992) calculated effect sizes "attributable to parent involvement" for a number of studies conducted during the 1970s. Although effect sizes ranged from "negative" in three studies to 1 to 2 standard deviations in another dozen studies, it was found that the most carefully designed (and therefore the most defensible) studies produced small, often nonsignificant effects of a parent-based component. Given the methodological weaknesses of many intervention evaluations, White and others concluded that the research evidence does not support the generalization that adding a parent component to a child-focused program produces greater immediate gains in children's cognitive achievements.

Even if the immediate benefits of adding a parent component to an intervention are not always obvious, the long-term effects may be quite beneficial. In his review of early childhood intervention programs, Bronfenbrenner (1974) reported that chldren "in most home-based programs not only made substantial initial gains, but these gains increased and continued to hold up rather well three to four years after the intervention had been discontinued" (p. 291). He concluded that "without family involvement, intervention is likely to be unsuccessful, and what few effects are achieved are likely to disappear once the intervention is discontinued" (p. 300).

Several explanations have been proposed to account for the relative effectiveness of educational programs with a home-based component, compared to those with a school-based component only. First, there are clear advantages to enlisting the mother (or other family member) as the primary agent of change since interactions between parents and children involve emotional as well as cognitive components, within the context of strong and enduring interpersonal relationships. Second, parents are able to work individually with their children and adapt their interactions to the child's needs and special interests, while teachers must be concerned with pacing a group of students. Third, by involving the family, home-based interventions can begin very early in the child's life, during the critical years of rapid development when small changes in environmental stimulation and support can yield significant improvements in children's performance on cognitive tasks (Wachs and Gruen, 1982). Fourth, parent education and support programs can help parents improve their own lives, increasing their self-confidence and motivation to pursue education or job training and increasing their abilities to serve as advocates for themselves and their children (Cochran and Dean, 1991).

Fifth, as Bronfenbrenner (1974) has pointed out, if changes have been incorporated into the home and into ongoing family interactions, the "treatment" continues after the formal intervention ceases. Researchers conducting longitudinal evaluations of the effects of early intervention programs have noted that the educational experiences and processes that the child encounters after the program play a critical role in determining whether the initial benefits of program participation will persist or deteriorate (Lazar and others, 1977). If changes are incorporated into the home learning environment, parents can provide experiences and encouragement to reinforce and supplement their children's school experiences. Such support may sustain children whose school experiences are not optimal.

Sixth, in this situation, not only will the targeted child benefit but other members of the household, for example, younger siblings, may also benefit from the changes parents make in the home learning environment, creating a multiplier or "diffusion" effect from the initial program (Goodson and Hess, 1976; Gray and Klaus, 1970). There is every likelihood that skills learned by parents to deal with older children will be used with younger children without further intervention (van Leer Foundation, 1986). Finally, a home-based intervention increases the congruence between the demands and expectations of the home and the school, with the result that home experiences reinforce rather than detract from school experiences (Comer, 1984; Peters, Bollin, and Murphy, 1991).

These conclusions assume that significant and substantial changes have been made in the home learning environment as a result of parent education or home intervention. Surprisingly, relatively few studies have assessed changes in home processes. More often than not, the emphasis of earlier studies was on the *product* (student achievement) rather than the *process* (parent-child interactions). More recently, some researchers have been devoting more attention to the type and degree of change that may take place in the home learning environment following parent education and home intervention. We turn now to an examination of the effects of these programs on parent variables and home processes.

Effects on Parent and Home Variables

Several studies have noted improvements in parents' "sense of control" over their own lives and their self-confidence in guiding their children's learning and development (see Clarke-Stewart and Apfel, 1978; Gray and Wandersman, 1980; Zigler and Berman, 1983). This was achieved by providing models and confidants to work with parents (Gordon, 1973; Lasater, Malone, and Ferguson, 1976), through peer support in discussion groups (Slaughter, 1983), or by helping parents develop social networks and support systems (Kessen and Fein, 1975). Programs based on a philosophy of "empowering" parents have demonstrated notable improvements in parents' self-confidence and self-esteem, their perceptions of themselves as parents, and their ties to a larger social network for support and resources (for example, Cochran and Dean, 1991). Changes in parents' attitudes toward their roles in their children's learning may result in parents becoming more confident and less authoritarian in their child-rearing practices (Clarke-Stewart and Apfel, 1978) and may also translate into more flexible and realistic expectations for their children's development (Lasater, Malone, and Ferguson, 1976; Leler and others, 1975).

Parental attitudes toward school and school personnel have been improved through school-directed programs to increase the amount (or quality) of communication between parents and teachers (Becher, 1984; Becker and Epstein, 1982; Epstein, 1986; Herman and Yeh, 1983). Some evidence suggests that improved parental attitudes toward school are accompanied by increased parental involvement in children's school activities (Epstein, 1986, 1987b) and by an increase in the range of topics that parents are willing to discuss with teachers (Powell, 1978). Although the direct benefits to the child are unclear, parental support for school personnel may be conveyed to the child in a variety of subtle ways, thereby reinforcing the value of schooling and of doing well there.

In a study of parents enrolled in Family Math classes, Sloane (1989a, 1989b) found notable shifts in parents' attitudes toward the subject area, in their beliefs about their children's learning in mathematics, and in their own knowledge and awareness of effective strategies for encouraging their children's interests and skills in mathematics. At the end of the six- to eight-week course, changes in parents' knowledge and attitudes were more evident than were changes in parents' behaviors and math-related interactions with their children at home, but preliminary data from interviews with parents three to six months later suggested that behavioral changes may follow. If so, such findings would be consistent with Hess's (1981) proposition that parental attitudes and beliefs serve as "cognitive mediators," shaping and guiding parents' decisions regarding their interactions with their children.

Evidence of marked changes in families as a result of intervention is to be found in the Thai study described previously (Janhom, 1983). In this study, the processes of each home were assessed using scales developed by Davé (1963) before the intervention began and again on its completion. Over the six-month period of the study, parents in all experimental groups showed significant changes in home process variables compared to parents who had not participated in any form of home intervention. Further, the children who gained most in achievement came from families who had demonstrated the greatest change in home processes. That is, student gains in achievement corresponded directly to changes in the degree of family support for school learning.

Other programs have been designed to alter the teaching behaviors of parents by teaching them "pedagogically sound" strategies for instructing their children in the development of tasks and skills. In an analysis of four evaluation studies related to the Parent Education Follow-Through Project, Olmsted and

Rubin (1982) reported that parents did gain competence in using specific "desirable teaching behaviors" in a laboratory setting and were able to apply the teaching principles in subsequent interactions with their children (for example, by asking children more questions that required them to use "high-order" mental processes to answer).

In preschool programs, aspects of verbal interaction between parent and child are perhaps the most common variables of interest in research. Programs may focus on increasing the quantity or number of verbal interactions (by encouraging parents to verbalize more during play, for example) or they may focus on increasing parents' use of more complex or elaborated language with their children (Kessen and Fein, 1975; Levenstein, 1970). The responsiveness of parents during these verbal interactions is of particular interest in many programs, but the results are mixed. In one program, for example, Slaughter (1983) found that mothers did become more nurturing, receptive, and responsive during their interactions with their children; but in their review of preschool programs, Clarke-Stewart and Apfel (1978) concluded that although the programs may be effective in improving the number of parental verbal interactions, they are much less effective in improving parental responsiveness, playfulness, or affection in these interactions.

Relative Alterability of Home Process Variables

Several investigators have noted that not all aspects of homes are equally affected by participation in parent involvement programs. Clarke-Stewart and Apfel (1978) concluded that it was more difficult to alter affective and attitudinal variables than behavioral variables, such as patterns of verbal interaction. MacPhee, Ramey, and Yeates (1984) found it easier to increase parents' knowledge of effective strategies or child-rearing practices than to influence their beliefs and attitudes toward their children's learning. In contrast, Sloane (1989b) documented immediate changes in attitudinal variables but found behavioral variables more resistant to change over the short term. Because of the different methods and approaches employed in studies, generalizations about the extent to which homes can be changed have proven difficult.

Janhom (1983) directly addressed the issue of alterability in his home intervention study. Regardless of the method of parent education (that is, parent meeting groups, home visits, or provision of newsletters), similar patterns were found in the relative degree to which changes occurred in specific home variables. A comparison of specific aspects of the home environment before and after intervention indicated that some variables were amenable to change over the six-month period, while other variables remained stable and resistant to change.

The variables that Janhom found to be most alterable related to academic guidance and support and academic aspirations and expectations. It would seem that parents' opinions and attitudes toward children's school learning can be changed over time if parents receive information or evidence that motivates such changes. Similarly, providing specific information on materials and strategies for reinforcing school lessons can increase the availability, quality, and frequency of the academic guidance and support that parents give their children. Variables relating to the language environment of the home proved most resistant to change. Since the quality of parents' use of language has been strongly established for a long time, we should not be too surprised to find that it is not easily or readily changed. Other home process variables showed some degree of alterability. Although parents often could not provide learning materials (such as books, magazines, mass media) or toys, games, and hobbies that could be used to explore and discuss ideas and events, they were able to provide opportunities for thinking and imagining. In general, although parents were resistant to changing the established structure and routines of the home, they were prepared to opt for more educational activities when the beneficial effect of such activities was demonstrated.

Peters, Bollin, and Murphy (1991) also documented changes in several home processes, including significant increases in the provision of toys and reading materials, following participation in a parent involvement program. The most pronounced changes occurred when parents had one-on-one contact with a home visitor. Efforts to improve the availability and use of resources in the home may also be enhanced when parents can take home materials, as in "make and take" workshops or "lending libraries" offered by a program. Showing parents how to use everyday household items or how to take advantage of existing family activities to reinforce concepts and skills are other ways to improve intellectual stimulation in the home without placing additional financial burdens on families.

Program Characteristics and Outcomes

It has proven difficult to isolate the effects of specific program characteristics on either child or parent variables. As Goodson and Hess (1976) noted: "[It is] easier to produce effects in intervention programs than to identify the specific factors which contribute to success" (p. 257). Henderson (1984) concluded that the form of parent involvement may not be critical as long as it is reasonably well planned, comprehensive, and long lasting. Although many program characteristics do not seem to relate to the effectiveness of a program as measured by improvements in children's cognitive performance or achievement, the content of a parent education program, its philosophical approach, and the expertise of staff all seem to be consistently related to program outcomes (Clarke-Stewart and Apfel, 1978; Goodson and Hess, 1976). However, the appropriate research has not been done to verify this conclusion.

Further, a number of specific program characteristics seem to be generally more effective than others. Programs that provide more structure and concrete activities seem to be more effective than ones that attempt to teach "general principles" of parent-child interaction (Goodson and Hess, 1976). Some researchers have emphasized the importance of linking the information presented in parent education to the parents' own experiences and everyday lives (Luscher, 1977, cited in Florin and Dokecki, 1983). One way to provide concrete activities and to help parents integrate information into their own interactions with their children is to give parents the opportunity to work with their children in the parent education program. The length of the program also seems to be important (Florin and Dokecki, 1983; Stevens, 1978). Longer programs may not produce higher immediate gains than shorter programs, but consistency and followup can yield longer-lasting changes in the home environment.

Not surprisingly, the extent to which parents can apply the principles and strategies taught in a home intervention program is directly related to the success of the program. In a review of forty-eight studies of educational programs involving parents, Leler (1983) found that the more comprehensive and intensive the level of parent involvement, the more effective were the results. In an experimental kindergarten program for disadvantaged children, Irvine (1979) found that the degree to which parents were involved (measured simply by the number of hours parents participated in school and home visits, meetings, and the like) was directly related to children's scores on tests of general reasoning and verbal concepts. The relationships between parent involvement and children's achievements were highly significant, even after controlling for other factors, such as levels of family education and income or children's ages and previous performance.

Evidence from other studies also supports the conclusion that programs that allow maximum interaction, either between the parent and the parent educator or among parents, tend to produce more positive results. For example, Janhom (1983) and Slaughter (1983) each found that parents who participated in group meetings with other parents made greater changes in the home learning environment than did parents who received only home visits or written materials. The fact that group meetings allow parents to share ideas and develop support networks with other parents may be a critical factor in encouraging them to try new strategies with their children at home. Other investigators, however, have found that, for some parents, one-to-one contact between the parent and the parent educator is most helpful (for example, Cochran and Woolever, 1983).

Other factors shown to influence parents' reactions to and home applications of home intervention programs are the parents' views of how valid or "meaningful" the content of the program is; the compatibility between program goals and parents' own values and beliefs; the emphasis on parents' sense of responsibility as the primary educator of their children; the parents' styles of participation (whether or not they interact with their peers, for example); and the extent to which parents have a support system of family and friends (see Clarke-Stewart and Appel, 1978; Goodson and Hess, 1976; Kessen and Fein, 1975). We would expect the characteristics of parents (for example, their social and economic circumstances, education, motivation) to influence the degree and type of their participation in programs as well as what they gain from their participation. But again, systematic research on the topic is limited. In Powell's (1986) review of existing evidence on the relationships between parent characteristics and program participation, he noted that program participation was affected by personality factors (for example, parents' disposition to be expressive or controlled), parents' self-confidence and sense of control over their own lives, and the extent and strength of parents' existing social network and kinship ties. Powell and others have called for more research on how to match program characteristics and structure to meet the needs and characteristics of parents.

Conclusion

The research reviewed in this chapter leads to the conclusion that the effects of home intervention and parent education programs can be quite impressive. Numerous comprehensive reviews of the results of such programs over the years indicate that efforts to help parents become stronger partners in their children's learning can have a significant positive impact on children's cognitive development, school performance, and social functioning. However, there are at least three areas in which further research is needed to improve our understanding of the effects of parent education and home intervention.

First is the area of family support programs. Comprehensive programs that address a variety of parents' and children's needs seem promising, but there is relatively little systematic research on these programs to date. Comprehensive programs are difficult to evaluate, given the number of variables and possible sources of influence and the emphasis on individualizing the "treatment" for each family. However, these programs represent important efforts to address the needs of families in all parts of the world who are coping with the demands of modern society and the stresses induced by poverty. We need to understand better what can and cannot be accomplished in such programs.

Second, we still do not fully understand the relationships between parent characteristics, program characteristics, and the effects of program participation on parents and children. Although researchers have called for more work in this area for many years, the question of "what works best for whom" is rarely addressed in most evaluations. Understanding the influence of the variety of factors that are likely to affect the degree to which parents participate in and benefit from parent education can only improve our ability to design more effective programs.

And third, more research is needed on the extent to which programs produce changes in home environments and how these changes relate to subsequent changes in child variables. We do not adequately understand which variables can be changed most readily and under what conditions. More research in this area should not only improve the design of parent education programs but should also contribute to a better understanding of the ways in which children draw upon the environment to construct their knowledge, attitudes, and skills in a given domain of learning.

The many successful programs now in operation should be studied carefully to increase our understanding of the processes that make them successful. Such studies would provide invaluable information on the critical elements of effective interventions and would offer a "template" that could be adapted to fit the needs and resources of specific groups, communities, or parents. At this stage, we need to move forward from the question of whether interventions work toward questions of how we might develop more efficient, cost-effective, and feasible strategies that educators can use to encourage all parents to become more effective partners in their children's learning.

The Foundations ▪ EIGHT
of Scholastic
Development

The programs to help parents encourage and support their children's learning that were described in Chapters Six and Seven focused on a wide range of concepts and skills necessary for scholastic achievement. In this chapter, we describe the cognitive and noncognitive characteristics that we believe underlie many of these concepts and skills and that therefore seem especially important for school success. We also indicate how parents and other family members play a critical role in the development of these characteristics. We believe that an awareness of this role should help family members in their efforts to promote child development and school success.

Cognitive Characteristics

Children's learning at school is usually described in terms of competence in the subject areas around which the work of school is organized—reading, mathematics, science, social science, a second language. However, it seems likely that learning in all these domains is based on a variety of more fundamental elements. Some of these elements are specific to particular subjects or tasks and involve specialized knowledge, skills, and affects. Others are more general and are used over and over in a variety of school-learning tasks. Support for this view can be found in an examination of relationships between performances

on standardized tests of ability and on tests of achievement in
school, which yield correlations of about .5 over a variety of
courses and subject areas (Lavin, 1965). The magnitude of these
relationships is large enough to suggest that the performances
are based on knowledge and skills common to the two types of
test but small enough to indicate that some aspects of the performances are due to knowledge and skills specific to each area
of ability or achievement.

In this chapter, our concern will be with the former—
that is, with the general knowledge and information-processing
skills and strategies that seem to underlie performance on a variety of school-related tasks and achievements. Various attempts
have been made to describe the nature of such knowledge, skills,
and strategies and how individuals build them up through experience and consolidate them over time (see Snow, 1982; Sternberg, 1985). Bruner (1985), for example, posits that in their early
years, through interactions with their environment, children
"construct" a range of sensorimotor, perceptual, and cognitive
structures that provide them with a "model" of their world. Such
models may be described in terms of three major components:
concepts, propositions, and schemata (Wickelgren, 1979). The
concept, of which there are many types, is the basic unit of information. Some concepts can be described as "concrete" (for example, a table, a ball), others as "abstract" (for example, freedom, energy). The relationship of two or more concepts, which
can take place in a variety of more-or-less complex ways, leads
the child to *propositions.* As in the case of concepts, propositions
can also vary in their degree of abstractness and in their content. Some contain factual information (The dog is very big),
others describe procedural knowledge (If you want to turn on
the light, you have to press the switch), while others describe
relations in terms of predictability (If I let the glass fall, it will
probably break).

Just as concepts are interrelated, so are propositions. The
interrelationship of a number of propositions is called a *schema.*
The schema provides an organizational structure in which relationships between concepts and propositions are represented.
It contains the information that we have accumulated through

experience of interrelationships between objects, events, and sequences of events as they normally occur. It allows us, for example, to infer causation — that when certain conditions exist, something else invariably follows.

Although we have described the knowledge, skills, and strategies that children build up over time in terms of concepts, propositions, and schemata, there are other ways to describe cognitive capacities. But of greater importance than the precise terms one might use is to appreciate that children must structure information, integrate it with other information, and develop the ability to identify underlying principles, patterns, and relationships, since it is those operations that enable them to interpret new situations and that facilitate problem solving and learning. Such organization also allows relevant knowledge to be located in memory and, when it is needed, to be applied in new situations. Conversely, when one is unable to access knowledge because of inadequate organization or structure, one is likely to experience difficulties in learning new material (Glaser, 1987).

If cognitive development consists of gradually building up and organizing a store of concepts, propositions, and schemata that can be applied in a variety of contexts, then we have further evidence to that presented in Chaper One of its cumulative nature. One cannot establish schemata unless one has previously established propositions; propositions, in turn, depend on the earlier acquisition of concepts. Vygotsky (1978) demonstrated this cumulative nature of development in a more concrete way when he showed that children's initial mastery of basic arithmetical operations provides the basis for the subsequent development of a variety of highly complex thinking processes.

Another important feature of children's cognitive development is the movement, in thought and language, from the ablty to deal with the concrete present to the ability to deal with what is more remote and abstract. At a very early age, as children come to perceive many aspects of the world around them, development relies heavily on sensory modalities, such as vision, hearing, touch, taste, and smell. Development continues in more and more complex ways as children approach the beginning of formal schooling at the age of five or six. Although the learning that takes place as a result of actual physical contact with objects in the environment (for example, exploring the properties of objects and discovering that they are hard or heavy or break easily) is important for children, it really is only the beginning of a series of learning tasks that must be accomplished in the course of development. Increasingly, as children grow older, their learning becomes less concrete and less contextualized; it comes to depend more and more on their ability to construct and use models of the environment in their own heads.

In time, children learn, in their thinking and talking, to deal not just with physically present objects or current activities but also with absent objects or past and future activities. They also learn to converse with unfamiliar partners and to estimate what their listeners are likely to know. These instances of children's decreased reliance on the present or the historical context of interaction may be taken as evidence of growing abstraction and increased decontextualization in their thought (Snow, 1983).

Of all the skills that children bring to school, the importance of verbal skills for future learning has repeatedly been stressed. This view is supported by evidence that children's verbal ability is closely related to school achievement. For example, one aspect of verbal ability, knowledge of vocabulary, has been found to be one of the best predictors of reading achievement in the first grade (Bloom, 1976). The importance of language for cognitive development becomes clear when we realize that as children come to perceive the world they are helped to "fix" or hold particular objects and events in mind by being given words or other symbols to attach to them. *Mama* and *Dada* come to represent important adults while *bottle, cap,* and *dog* become symbols for other objects. Other words, such as *under, over, before,* and *after* provide the framework for establishing propositions that describe relationships between objects and events.

As children develop more complex language, they improve their ability to perceive aspects of the environment and to abstract such aspects and fix them in memory, leading to a general increase in their control over the environment. The frequent use of language in relation to the physical environment and to people also enables children to use language to express emotions, intentions, and desires. It helps them too in considering alternatives with regard to their emotions and in developing ways of delaying gratification of desires (Bloom, 1981).

Literacy, which some children acquire at home and others do not, is particularly relevant to school success, since so much school work involves activities and skills associated with reading and writing. It would appear that certain conditions in the home contribute to the development of both oral language (speaking and listening) and literacy (reading and writing). For example, both are supported by patterns of interaction with adults that involve a pedagogical component. This component is apparent in the acquisition of oral language when parents (or other adults) focus on the content of children's speech, add new information to a topic, ask questions that require children to clarify what they've said, or answer children's questions. Analogous processes can be detected in the domain of literacy; for example, when a parent (or other adult) carries on a conversation with the child about the text or pictures in books or asks or answers questions about the meaning of words. Such activities have been found to be related to reading achievement at the preschool level.

If the conditions necessary for the development of oral language are similar to those necessary for the development of literacy, why do the vast majority of children develop adequate oral language skills but a considerable proportion have difficulty acquiring literacy skills? The answer sometimes given to this question is that although literacy and oral language are related they involve somewhat different skills. If this is so, then it would not be surprising to find greater variation in one than in the other. Snow's (1983) explanation of the fact that some children are less successful in acquiring literacy than oral language again underlies the importance of developing the ability to abstract from present situations and to decontextualize information. For according to Snow, it is the child's failure to develop the ability to decontextualize information that underlies literacy difficulties. This failure becomes particularly important and apparent in the middle primary school grades when students, having learned to decode and comprehend print, are faced with the tasks of reading from textbooks or writing clear paragraphs.

Noncognitive Characteristics

Noncognitive characteristics are important aspects of children's development not only in their own right but also because they may play a critical role in the development of cognitive characteristics and school learning. By the same token, it seems likely that cognitive characteristics affect the development of noncognitive characteristics.

A variety of noncognitive characteristics have been examined in research relating to children's school achievement. In many cases, the characteristics involved and the ways in which they are measured are less precise than in the case of cognitive achievements. Nevertheless, research has identified many interesting relationships between school achievement and noncognitive variables.

One cluster of noncognitive variables comprises children's self-concepts, which include feelings of self-esteem, self-efficacy or ability to control one's destiny, and ego-resiliency (Harter, 1983). General self-esteem can be defined as the evaluation an individual makes and customarily maintains with regard to himself or herself (Dolan, 1981). Many studies indicate that students with high self-esteem do better at school than children with low self-esteem. For example, Coleman and others (1966) found that a measure of students' evaluation of their own ability predicted between 5 and 10 percent of variance in the verbal achievements of white American students at grades 6, 9, and 12. Children with high self-esteem also set themselves more realistic goals, are less upset by failure, and show less need for adult approval.

It is likely that more focused concepts of self than general self-esteem, such as academic self-concepts, are more closely related to school learning. In broad terms, academic self-concept is an individual's perception of himself or herself as a learner. People have feelings about themselves as learners in general and about their competence in specific areas of the curriculum (for example, mathematics, science, music) (Shavelson, Hubner, and Stanton, 1976). Such feelings have been found to account for up to 25 percent of variation in school achievement (Dolan, 1981).

Children's concepts about their ability to learn can have serious implications when it comes to learning new tasks. Take the case of Daniel, a ten-year-old child with learning difficulties. When asked to perform a laboratory task, Daniel responded by saying, "Is this a memory thing? Didn't they tell you I can't do this stuff? Didn't they tell you I don't have a memory?" (Brown, Bransford, Ferrara, and Campione, 1983). This is a good example of a case in which a child's effort to avoid a situation that taps a weakness results in a loss of experience in the very area in which it is needed. Further, it seems likely that in these circumstances the effort that should be directed to solving a problem is used to deal with the anxiety created by it. When children think that a problem is beyond their resources, it can have a paralyzing effect on learning.

The acquisition of a concept of one's academic self has been described as a key developmental task of middle childhood in modern society (Baker and Entwistle, 1987). It is a task that seems to be influenced by appraisals by others and by the social context of home and school.

When we talk about self-concept, we are talking about the self as a cognitive construction, one that is the object of evaluative scrutiny as the child develops. But the self also functions to control its own behavior (Harter, 1983). In considering this function, we see a good example of the role that cognitive factors play in the development of noncognitive areas, such as motivation and feelings of competence. In developing control, children must acquire, on the one hand, an understanding of who or what is responsible for the outcomes in their lives and, on the other, a belief that they are primarily responsible for their own behavior (Harter, 1983). The fact that individuals differ in their beliefs regarding their ability to control their lives has led investigators to distinguish between individuals for whom locus of control is internal and those for whom it is external.

People with internal locus of control believe that they can control their own behavior, personality, and effort; people with external locus of control see events, including their own behavior, as being determined by forces outside themselves (Lefcourt, 1976; Levenson, 1981).

Individuals who have strong internal control, compared to those who have not, have been found to be more cognitively active, to be more likely to delay gratification, and to have high task persistence. Such individuals are also likely to possess high levels of intrinsic motivation and self-reliance. And, as in the case of academic self-concept, locus of control has been found to predict up to 25 percent of variance in achievement in basic academic areas (reading, mathematics, language) of third through fifth graders (Dolan, 1981). In the large-scale study of Coleman and others (1966), a measure of sense of control of the environment accounted for up to 12 percent of variance in verbal achievement in grades 6, 9, and 12. In fact, in this study, a set of variables that included students' self-concept, sense of control of the environment, and interest in school accounted for more of the variance in student achievement than either a set of family background variables or a set of school characteristic variables.

When compared to white students, minority group students have been found to show a lower sense of control of their environment (Coleman and others, 1966). This is perhaps not surprising since many minority group students come from families where control of the environment is more limited than in the typical white home. Coleman and others concluded that, "for many disadvantaged children, a major obstacle to achievement may arise from the very way they confront the environment. Having experienced an unresponsive environment, the virtues of hard work, of diligent and extended effort toward achievement appear to such a child unlikely to be rewarding" (p. 321). This view has much in common with the views of Ogbu (1987) regarding minority group children, which we considered in our discussion of home-school discontinuities in Chapter Two.

It is a matter of debate whether the positive relationships that have been found between students' cognitive and noncognitive characteristics are to be taken as an indication that students' noncognitive characteristics contribute to the development of cognitive characteristics. On the assumption that this is so, Head Start and other programs for students in disadvantaged areas were designed to improve children's self-esteem in the hope that their achievements would also improve (Shavelson, Hubner, and Stanton, 1976). There is, however, an alternative explanation of the relationships found between students' cognitive and noncognitive characteristics: it is that noncognitive (in particular, affective) characteristics develop as a by-product of a students' success in the cognitive domain. That is, students who do well in the cognitive area will develop positive interests and attitudes toward it and positive images of themselves as learners (Bloom, 1975). It does not seem unreasonable to suppose that the influence goes both ways. For example, if children develop a positive self-image in the home, we would expect them to tackle school-learning tasks with confidence. And in time, children's success in school could be expected to evoke a positive perception of themselves as learners as well as positive feelings toward the work of school and what is accomplished there. Home support and encouragement play an important role in the development of such positive perceptions and feelings (Kifer, 1975).

The Role of the Home

During children's development, the physical and social interactions between them and their environment are obviously extremely complex. We would expect development to be affected by a number of factors. First, the range and type of stimuli in the children's environment seem crucial in determining the extent and direction of development. By stimuli we mean not just physical objects but also the knowledge and system of symbols that have been developed in the children's culture and family in response to physical, psychological, and social conditions. Every child finds that the environment has been interpreted and structured for him or her in certain ways by the culture and family, that certain aspects of the environment receive special attention, and that certain knowledge and skills are particularly valued. Many of the parent behaviors identified in research as predicting cognitive development relate to how parents organize and present aspects of the environment for their children. These include providing a variety of activities and experiences, ample play and conversation between parents and children, and opportunities for children to explore and to try out new skills and activities in meaningful settings (Rutter, 1985b). It is with such activities and experiences that the guidelines to promote cognitive development and school learning in Chapter Nine are concerned.

A second issue to consider in examining children's development is how children come to be directed toward and engage in certain activities rather than in others. In some cases, it seems that children are directed to activities that are rewarded in some way and are diverted from activities that are punished (see Williams, 1976). It is unlikely, however, that all of children's development is shaped through such a system of reinforcement.

A further factor (about which we know relatively little) is how the characteristics of individual children affect their interaction with the environment. There are many characteristics — in particular, children's level of development as represented in their levels of knowledge, skills, dispositions, and attitudes — that we would expect to be important in determining what will engage children and how they will react to the objects, persons, or ideas they encounter.

Although much remains to be learned about all these factors, the general principle that the home plays a central role in the development of the cognitive and noncognitive characteristics described in this chapter is hardly in question. In the noncognitive area, if it is true that the development of attitudes, self-concept, and motivation requires an environment in which involvement between individuals is intense and intimate and in which personal attention and interest are individualized, consistent, and sustained over time, then it would seem clear that the role of the home is crucial. It is not surprising that research evidence points to the fact that self-esteem has its roots in children's preschool experiences in the family and among peers (Harter, 1983). Children whose esteem is high have received more attention, affection, and encouragement from their parents than have children with low esteem. Low self-esteem, however, can also develop when children are at school. This can happen if children are frequently faced with tasks they cannot accomplish, giving rise to a situation in which the children become aware of their failure to perform adequately. In these circumstances, some children develop poor self-esteem; others reject schooling as irrelevant or boring. In either case, they are unlikely to make satisfactory progress in school learning.

While the structure, size, and functions of families are conducive to providing children with an environment in which they receive sustained and individualized attention, the structure, size, and functions of other institutions, including the school, are not. Given the objectives of schools and the fact that interpersonal relationships in them lack closeness, intimacy, and individualization, it is difficult to see how they could perform the family's traditional functions of nurturing the development of children's noncognitive characteristics. It follows from this that if many families today, because of a variety of societal and familial changes, have been weakened in their child-rearing functions (as was noted in Chapter Five), efforts to remedy this should be directed primarily toward the family and other individuals and institutions that might be able to provide conditions approximating those of the family. In this context, informal support networks among parents and other forms of peer group support seem particularly appropriate.

In considering characteristics that are more obviously cognitive, the role of the home again seems paramount. During the preschool years, it is the home that can most obviously provide stimulating environments, rich in the range of experiences available, which make use of games, toys, and many other objects for manipulation, and in which there is frequent interaction between children and adults at meals, playtime, and throughout the day. As children grow older, they need opportunities for learning about not just the physical conditions of the here-and-now but also the world of ideas and the larger environment beyond the home in time and space. Children's ability to abstract and decontextualize information is likely to be assisted by parents (and other adults) when they engage in progressively more complex activity with their children, when they help children recount events and build internal representations of those events, when they tell or read stories in which the author is impersonal, and when positions have to be understood from the point of view of different persons (Bronfenbrenner, 1979; Snow, 1983).

More experienced members of the culture (adults or more capable peers) have a further role to play, by determining that the level of difficulty of tasks that children engage in is appropriate to their developmental level. According to Vygotsky (1978), children develop their thinking capabilities by engaging in tasks that are somewhat beyond their present level. If the task is too easy, the children will not learn anything new. But if the task is too difficult, then (in the terminology of the present chapter) the children's present store of concepts, propositions, and schemata will not be adequate to deal with it. A judgment of difficulty in this situation is crucial, and it is one that can only be made by a more experienced individual who is closely attuned to the child's developmental level.

Piaget (1950) has stressed the importance of social collaboration for children's intellectual development for other reasons. For Piaget, the main trend in the development of intelligence is toward decentralization of the thought processes, a freeing of the individual's perceptions and thoughts from egocentricity. Again, the assistance of more mature individuals is indicated. "It is precisely by a constant interchange of thought with others that we are able to decentralize ourselves in this way, to coordinate internally relations deriving from different viewpoints" (p. 164). The social foundations of logical thought are obvious in this view, since individuals are judged to arrive at logic as the result of cooperation and the free interchange of ideas with other people.

In developing increasingly complex and abstract models of their environments, the precise model (concepts, propositions, and schemata) that children will develop will depend less on the characteristics of their physical environment than on the knowledge and system of symbols that are available to them. Here we may recall that, in the context of a discussion of discontinuities between home and school in Chapter Two, for children from certain backgrounds much of what they learn in the home and in the community may differ from what they learn at school. In the terminology of the present chapter, we can say that communities and families may differ from schools in the concepts, propositions, and schemata that they possess and pass on to their children.

Although some homes may not foster the particular knowledge and abilities that facilitate learning at school and may vary in the assistance they give their children to develop these abilities, this should not be taken to mean that these homes are not capable of, or are opposed to, doing so. If assistance were provided to these parents and if they believed that it would help prepare their children for school, many would be willing to enlarge the range of their children's experience and to adopt a variety of strategies to promote their children's learning.

If much learning is regarded as "a dynamic social event that depends upon a minimum of two heads, one better informed or more skilled than the other" (Belmont, 1989), then children are going to require help from one or more of a variety of people with whom they come into contact — mothers, but also fathers, grandparents, brothers, sisters, and family friends. Such help is not always formal or structured. Some learning occurs simply through observation and perhaps imitation of the behavior of more mature people in everyday social interaction. Many routine activities, including language, seem to be learned in this informal way. In other cases, somebody adopts a more didactic approach and so, for example, corrects a child's language or explains that certain actions have certain consequences (for example, If you go too near the fire, you will get burned). The didactic approach may become even more formal, as when somebody sets out to teach a child some particular knowledge or skill (for example, to play a musical instrument).

In this last case, one is coming close to the didactic approach of schools. Although homes do not normally adopt the formal teaching methods of the classroom, sometimes there are aspects of school teaching that parents use to provide home learning experiences for their children.

One such aspect involves the organization and structuring of information. Like schools, homes can help children by providing material that is organized in such a way that children can easily assimilate it into their collection of existing concepts, propositions, and schemata. Parents can also help children reorganize and restructure their existing knowledge in light of new information by pointing out similarities between the new information and what children already know.

While much of children's learning outside school is spontaneous, unplanned, and incidental, at times it can be helpful to introduce a more purposeful and systematic approach to a learning task. In particular, children will find it helpful in school if they have at least begun to learn how to pay attention to the particular aspects of a task that are relevant, rather than being impulsive and capricious in their reactions, and if they can concentrate on a task in hand long enough to become familiar with it and to organize the material that must be learned.

Conclusion

In this chapter, we discussed some of the cognitive and noncognitive characteristics that have been identified as important to the tasks of school learning. We saw that the development of these characteristics reflects opportunities that are available in children's homes and communities; that the early foundations of learning are important for later development; and that learning is cumulative. Social interactions between children and more experienced individuals play a key role in this development, and language plays a key role in promoting cognitive development and school success.

All these factors point to the home as the institution with the greatest opportunities to nurture the concepts, propositions, and schemata required for school learning, as well as the appropriate attitudes and orientations toward school and learning. Indeed, the development of many noncognitive characteristics that underlie learning, such as attitudes, self-concept, and motivation, would appear to require the peculiar conditions that normally only homes can provide — close intimate relationships that are stable and consistent over time. Further, it is also in the home that the child is likely to get the help it needs from older, more knowledgeable individuals in developing cognitive as well as noncognitive characteristics.

It should be clear from this chapter that in its role in children's development, the home should not be considered auxiliary, merely providing supplementary support for the work of the school. On the contrary, the home has to be recognized as the primary focus of learning, providing opportunities to foster children's development that are not normally available in other institutions. There are several aspects of the one-to-one relationships that exist in homes that parents (or other adults) might exploit to promote children's learning and development. First, parents (or other individuals) should take account of the development level of children when choosing learning tasks, ensuring that a task is neither too easy nor too difficult. Second, parents should deal with problems of confidence, anxiety, and threat, which are usually more apparent in a one-to-one situation than when a child is one of a large number of learners. Third, parents should use feedback based on children's performance to decide whether to repeat information, rephrase it, or adopt a different approach. Fourth, in a one-to-one situation, children can be encouraged to concentrate on the task in question. And fifth, immediate and positive response to children's accomplishments should help reinforce and consolidate learning (Brown, Bransford, Ferrara, and Campione, 1983). Even though children differ from each other in the level of support they need, parents will find that these aspects are likely to apply at one stage or another to the learning of all children.

NINE ◼ A Process-Based Approach for Homes

In Chapter Four, we described the findings of research that set out to identify conditions in homes associated with children's school learning. In this chapter, we draw on that research to develop and frame processes covering a range of home conditions and activities that relate to learning. The process variables can be categorized under five headings.

1. *Work Habits of the Family:* The degree of routine in the management of the home, the emphasis on regularity in the use of space and time, and the priority given to schoolwork over other pleasurable activities.
2. *Academic Guidance and Support:* The availability and quality of the help and encouragement that parents give their children in their schoolwork and the conditions they provide to support schoolwork.
3. *Stimulation to Explore and Discuss Ideas and Events:* Opportunities provided by the home to explore ideas, events, and the larger environment.
4. *Language Environment:* Opportunities in the home for the development of the correct and effective use of language.
5. *Academic Aspirations and Expectations:* Parents' aspirations for their children, the standards they set for children's school achievement, and their interest in and knowledge of children's school experiences.

These processes can be broken down into more specific characteristics, and ratings can be made of each on the basis of data obtained by interview and observation. As we saw in Chapter Four, when an overall index of the home environment based on these variables is related to children's performance on a scholastic ability test (Wolf, 1964) or on a battery of school achievement tests (Davé, 1963), the relationships are very high. Further, as we saw in Chapter Seven, clear educational benefits ensue when a parent education program such as the one proposed in this chapter helps parents enhance the educational aspects of their homes (Janhom, 1983).

We will now look in some more detail at the specific parent-child interactions that have great effect on children's school learning. In doing this, the most positive characteristics of these interactions are emphasized. In the Davé (1963) study and in other studies that followed this, the parents who emphasized these interactions had children who were highly successful in their school learning. The parents who rarely emphasized these interactions had children who were least successful.

Work Habits of the Family

Some degree of structure and routine in the home is essential to develop good work habits in the school as well as out of it. The Davé (1963) study found that children from homes with clear structure, shared responsibilities, and set routines learned better in school than children from homes where everyone did whatever they wanted to do, whenever they wanted. Children need to have a time to study, a time to work, a time to eat, a time to play, and a time to sleep. Ideally, there should be some allocation of space in the home to these various activities, including a space to study in relative quiet.

Parents and children can determine how to improve the activities and habits of members of the family. Major aspects of this might include the following:

• *The Degree of Structure, Sharing, and Punctuality in Home Activities.* This includes clear plans for work and play, sharing duties and household chores among family members, and emphasizing tasks being done on time. Although it is to be expected that younger children will not be required to do the same tasks as older children, each child should have some share in home activities.

- *Emphasis on Regularity in the Use of Time and Space in the Home.* This includes allocation of time for the family to eat, sleep, play, work, and study or read. Some balance among these activities may need to be worked out so that television or play do not take precedence over other activities. It is also important to provide a place for study and reading, at least in those times when members of the household are expected to engage in such activities.
- *Priority Given to Schoolwork, Reading, and Other Educative Activities over Television and Other Recreation.* Ideally, schoolwork and reading should be done before play, watching television, or even other work. A sufficient amount of time needs to be given to schoolwork, reading, and other educative activities, even if it reduces the time for play, TV, or other recreation.

Academic Guidance and Support

School learning is a long and difficult process for most children. Unless there is a great deal of support and encouragement, children will find it difficult to maintain their interest in and commitment to learning. Almost every child encounters some very difficult problems in particular aspects of learning. Unless there is someone to help children over these special difficulties, they may despair of their ability to learn. It is usually in the home that children get the encouragement and assistance they need to deal with difficult learning problems.

Homes differ greatly in the amount of encouragement and support they afford children. However, unless there is someone (in the home, school, or the community) who can provide the support each child needs at various times, the child may find school to be difficult and unrewarding. There are a number of kinds of guidance and support that homes may give to children.

- *Frequent Encouragement of Children for Their Schoolwork.* This includes frequent praise and approval for good schoolwork. It may include speaking approvingly to others about what the children have accomplished in school and drawing the attention of family and friends to it. It may also include small gifts and rewards related to things the children do well. As someone has put it, "It is catching the child when he or she has done something good and giving recognition for it."
- *Parental Knowledge of Strengths and Weaknesses in Children's School Learning and Supportive Help When They Really Need It.* Parents must have detailed knowledge of what their children are learning and of their children's special strengths and weaknesses in each school subject. They must encourage children to do their best. They should also help with learning problems and, if necessary, supervise their children's homework, study, or schedule of activity.
- *Availability of a Quiet Place to Study with Appropriate Books, Reference Materials, and Other Learning Materials.* Children need a quiet place in which to study, a desk or table at which to work, and books, a dictionary, and possibly other reference material. However, the emphasis is on the use of these rather than on their quality or their mere presence in the home. Although all homes may not be able to supply a separate room and a great variety of learning material, many homes can provide a place for children to work and a quiet period during which the children can devote themselves to study or reading.

Stimulation to Explore and Discuss Ideas and Events

Although learning that takes place outside the school may be related to learning that takes place in school, it is not organized by school subjects and is less formal. It is usually related to the activities of other members of the family; to conversations and other interchanges within the family; to the games, hobbies, and special interests of family members; and to shared activities of the family in play, reading, and visits to libraries, museums, concerts, and other cultural activities. It should be kept in mind that these activities differ from those in school because they take place as the occasion arises and they rarely involve the deliberate teaching by one family member of another.

- *Family Interest in Hobbies, Games, and Other Activities of Educative Value.* It is important for family members to share their interest in hobbies, games, and other activities that have educative value. Where possible, preference should be given to these activities over activities that are primarily recreational. However, what is important is that the activities are shared among members of the family and that each family member finds the activity interesting.
- *Family Use and Discussion of Books, Newspapers, Magazines, and Television Programs.* Ideally, family members should all read and discuss the ideas, views, and subjects of their reading. Daily events, news, and selected television programs can have great value in stimulating discussion of matters that may be of great significance. It is especially valuable if all the family take part in these discussions and exchanges. What is most essential is that each family member have an opportunity to express and share ideas and views with others. The discussions should take place frequently and informally.
- *Frequent Use of Libraries and Museums and Engagement in Cultural Activities.* Ideally, all family members should have a library card that they use frequently. The family should visit museums, zoos, historical sites, and other places of interest. In addition, they should share and discuss music, art, plays or films, and other cultural activities. If families cannot visit museums and the like, they select and discuss television programs that serve the same purpose.

Language Environment

Much learning is based on the use of language. It is largely through listening, reading, talking, and writing that learning takes place, inside the school and out. Language is used to store ideas in the mind and to recall them when required. Language is also used to share ideas and feelings with others. All individuals (at all ages) need to improve their language constantly and to use it more effectively. The home is where children learn much of their "mother tongue" and it is the place where they may have the greatest opportunity to enlarge and enrich language. The learning of language and its use in the home include the following:

- *Family Concern and Help for Correct and Effective Use of Language.* The family can provide great support for children's use of correct and effective language by emphasizing the development of good language habits. Family members can help children use the correct words and phrases needed to communicate with others. Where possible, family reading should be emphasized and the dictionary should be one of the most frequently used books in the home.
- *Opportunities for the Enlargement of Vocabulary and Sentence Patterns.* All members of the family should have some opportunity to talk about the day's events at the dinner table or on some other daily occasion when the family gathers. Each one should have some opportunity to speak and be listened to by other members of the family. The emphasis should be on ways in which each individual can communicate thoughts and feelings through an expanding and accurate use of the spoken language.

Academic Aspirations and Expectations

The home is usually the place where children secure the motivation to learn and to aspire to an education and life-style that will serve them well in the future. Typically, it is the parents who support and encourage their children at the different stages of their educational and cultural development. Almost no one can "make it" alone; each needs the support and encouragement of others to reach for higher goals in education and personal development. Although parents are usually central to this support, other family members may also provide encouragement. Some of the ways in which this can be done follow.

- *Parental Knowledge of Children's Current Schoolwork and School Activities.* Parents should know their children's current teacher(s), how the children are doing in school, the subjects being studied, and the learning materials being used. Parents should be interested in knowing about and sharing current school learning with their children. Also, parents need to know how well their children are doing and the subjects in which progress is good as well as subjects where special support may be needed.
- *Parental Standards and Expectations for Children's Schoolwork.* It is parents who usually set the standards for their children's learning in and out of school. Standards relate to the quality of the work children are expected to do as well as the grades or marks they should seek. However, parents should not only set standards but should also provide the support and even the direct help that children need when they do not meet these standards. This typically requires constant attention and communication, not just a monthly or yearly review of how well the children are doing in school.
- *Parental Education and Vocational Aspirations for Children.* It is parents who help children aspire to a high level of education and vocation. They communicate the level of education and occupation they would like their children to aspire to in frequent discussions and plans for the future. They help children make plans for high school and college and to see present learning in relation to such future goals. Frequently, parents encourage their children to make friends with other children who are serious about education and who have similar long-term goals and aspirations. It is also parents who make sacrifices of time and money in pursuit of these aspirations.

Conclusion

The ideas proposed in this chapter for a home program to increase the involvement of parents in the education of their children should not be interpreted as a list of rules to be followed mechanically. Rather, they are general guidelines that should be adapted to the environment of the home in which they are applied and to the needs of the children involved.

Further, the kind of learning that the program is designed to support does not concern the specifics of reading or writing or any of the specialized areas that are taught in primary school. Rather, the learning that the home can most readily support is of a general nature, as described in Chapter Eight, that can be used over and over again in a variety of situations. The home's major contribution is helping children construct a range of sensorimotor, perceptual, and cognitive structures that will form the foundation of later school learning and will continue to support that learning when children are at school. Parents' contribution to this process comes through providing children with opportunities, encouragement, and support systems that permeate their lives and allow them to acquire concepts, propositions, and schemata based on a rich personal experience and on the accumulated experience of the community.

TEN ◼ Involving Parents in Educational Roles: Issues and Prospects

A basic premise of this book has been that although the nature and quality of children's educational experience and development are influenced by factors as diverse as government policy relating to educational provision and neighborhood values, the two institutions that impinge most directly on children are their home and their school. Indeed, many of the wider influences of society on children are mediated through the opportunities and experiences provided by these institutions, particularly the home.

Throughout this book, our focus has been on the role of the home rather than of the school in developing children's school-learning capabilities. We will now look back on the major findings of the research that underlie this focus and at the implications of the findings for strengthening parents' involvement in their children's education. We will then look forward to situations in which people interested in improving home-school relationships might use a program of the type described in this book. We will consider how the program might fit into a home and the aspects of home life that it might affect.

Implications of Research

The research on the role of home environments in school learning has a number of implications. First, the home environment is a most powerful factor in determining the school learning of

144

students—their level of school achievement, their interest in school learning, and the number of years of schooling they will receive. This position is supported by research findings not just in the United States but in a great many countries across the industrialized and developing world. Thus, parents and the home environment hold a major key to the learning of children.

Second, when home and school have divergent approaches to life and to learning, children are likely to suffer in their school learning. Conversely, when home and school have similar emphases on motivation and learning, children are likely to do well. Both home and school have roles to play in helping children bridge any discontinuities that exist between the approach of the home and that of the school.

Third, the socioeconomic level or cultural background of a home need not determine how well a child does at school. Parents from a variety of cultural backgrounds and with different levels of education, income, or occupational status can and do provide stimulating home environments that support and encourage the learning of their children. It is what parents do in the home rather than their status that is important.

Fourth, parents should be in a better position to decide what to do in their homes if they have some understanding of the home factors that affect their children's school learning and know something about what they can do to encourage and support that learning. It is also an advantage if they know what is expected of their children in school. Programs designed to assist parents in supporting and encouraging their children have been found to help children in their school learning. The findings of many studies indicate that the "curriculum" of the home can be developed to benefit children in their school learning.

Improving the Home-School Relationship

While home and school differ in many obvious ways—in their priorities, in the demands and expectations that they try to meet, in their distinctive ways of relating to children, and in some cases, in their culture and language—at the same time, both share a common objective: to ensure the optimal development of children. To achieve this objective, parents provide for children's physical needs and lay the foundations for and support of children's school learning. For their part, schools accept the obligation of providing a suitable environment and staff and an appropriate curriculum that corresponds to the needs, interests, and problems of participants.

For a variety of reasons, not all schools and not all families are successful in promoting optimal learning. For example, some families may have difficulty in meeting the basic nutritional needs of children and may need assistance from outside agencies. On a wider scale, there is extensive evidence to suggest that the effectiveness of many homes in providing conditions conducive to the educational development of children has declined in recent years because of a variety of changes in society and in family structure and function. Because of these changes, many families—whether traditional, two-career, or single parent—find it increasingly difficult to provide children with basic support for schooling. In some families, children can be regarded as being particularly at risk. Further, the number of children living in such conditions is predicted to grow in the coming decades.

There are many examples today of efforts supported by parents, teachers, school officials, and educators to strengthen the home-school relationship (Epstein, 1987a). Most teachers foster this relationship by sending information to students' homes about such matters as school schedules, rules, and goals, or by reporting on students' progress. More active participation by parents includes involvement in school management and decision making, attendance at parent-teacher conferences, and helping with extracurricular activities or fund raising. Parent involvement on such activities has been found to be associated with higher levels of school performance by their children (Stevenson and Baker, 1987). However, these activities are likely to involve only a minority of parents.

A more radical approach, and one that is likely to be taken up by a greater number of parents, involves assigning a "teaching" role to parents. This approach exhibits a variety of procedures to strengthen the family role and responsibility and to improve the understanding, care, and education of children. The teaching role of the parent may be exercised in the school or at home. In the school, it may involve workshops, discussion groups, and training sessions for parents, or parents may assist teachers and students with lessons in the classroom. An example of how a parent may help in the classroom is when a teacher teaches a skill to a small group of children and then parents supervise the practice of the skill with this group while the teacher moves on to another group. Such activity not only helps teachers, it also gives parents the opportunity of learning about the activities of the classroom, which they can reinforce with their own children at home.

Direct efforts have also been made to involve parents in learning activities with their children in their own homes. These efforts often focus on children considered to be at risk and may be supported by workshops and group meetings with parents or by visits to homes by teachers or other facilitators. The purpose of these activities is to help children develop cognitive abilities for adaptation in school, which in turn should serve to reduce the discontinuities in knowledge, skills, language, learning, and attitudes experienced by all children to some extent and by some children to a great extent when they move from home to school. Typically, parents are helped to develop their tutoring skills, to stimulate learning, to share reading with their children, or to encourage conversation and discussion between themselves and their children. In some cases, a contract may be signed by teacher and parents that specifies a particular role for the parent in connection with children's school lessons or activities (Becker and Epstein, 1982).

Parent programs have been found to have significant and positive effects on children's verbal ability, language, school-related knowledge and skills, and achievement in school subjects, especially when integrated into a network of community support. They have also been found to alter parents' attitudes, self-concepts, and behavior, and to affect other members of the family and ultimately the community in which the family lives.

The basic conditions for the activities proposed in Chapter Nine for a home program to increase the involvement of parents in the education of their children are available in the majority of homes. However, some parents may need help in appreciating the importance of what they do and the manner in which they structure their homes and their lives for the development of their children. They may also need to consider giving greater emphasis to some aspects of their interactions with their children. For example, although language development, most of which occurs in the home, is a crucial area of human development, parents may not appreciate the importance for children's development of the communications that take place between family members. They may not realize that it is important that children develop competence in a variety of forms of language (listening, speaking, reading, writing); that language should be used to meet a variety of needs; that language can be used to decontextualize information; and that literacy is most likely to develop if it evolves as an interpersonal process, based on functional utility in an environment in which the child sees "significant others" (parents, brothers, sisters) making effective use of language (Davidson, Lia, and Troyer, 1988; Snow, 1983).

It is clear that language is not something taught in formal or semiformal sessions with children several times a week. While parents certainly can be expected to engage in formal or semiformal "teaching" from time to time—for example, helping their children complete a task, explaining something to them, or listening to them read—their continual informal interactions with children are more important: simply talking to them about school and other matters in their lives, discussing something the children have read or seen on television, planning activities, or expressing interest in children's achievements. Interactions involving these activities with children are not limited to parents, of course. Other family members and members of the children's immediate community, as more mature and knowledgeable people, can all provide dynamic social occasions for learning in children. In many homes, grandparents, brothers and sisters, aunts and uncles, and child-care providers share this role.

The context in which these activities occur in the home is also important. Individual activities are likely to be more effective if they take place against a backdrop of structure, regularity, and predictability about household events. Further, the atmosphere of the home should be one in which it is clear that parents highly value scholastic achievement, something that is possible even if parents themselves did not receive the full benefits of a formal education. It should also be clear to children that not only is scholastic progress valued, it is expected of them.

While the objectives and styles of teaching in the home and the school differ greatly from each other, there are times, particularly as the child gets older, that home practice will begin to approximate that of school. This may happen, for example, as parents monitor or help children with homework assignments. But for the most part, the home will be concerned with providing opportunities that the school cannot.

When considering the application of a parent involvement program in a specific home, attention should be paid to home circumstances, the histories of parents and children, and relations between school and home. At this stage, it may quickly become obvious that a program is inappropriate. For example, the program proposed in this book would not be suitable for dealing with educational problems that arise from nutritional deficiencies or from serious family dysfunction. Such a situation would require more radical approaches. The program would appear most suitable for families who are meeting their children's basic needs but are interested in strengthening their support for their children's formal education.

In considering home circumstances, it may be apparent that books, newspapers, television, libraries, or museums are not available to children. The precise resources or materials that are used, however, are less important than the identification of activities that have educative value. In fact, parents should be encouraged to use materials that are readily available in the children's immediate environment, to build on the existing strengths and interests of the family, and to use available resources in the community. What is important is that parents expose their children to a wide range of learning opportunities and use those opportunities to develop children's knowledge and cognitive skills (R. W. Henderson, 1981).

It is important that the content of programs be adapted

to the developmental level of the child. Much of this will be done intuitively, based on parents' knowledge of their children. The activities suitable for a preschool child will not be the same as those for a high school student. Ideally, tasks should go a short distance in difficulty beyond the level of problem solving at which children can perform without assistance. If a task is too easy, children will not learn anything new by engaging in it and may become bored. If it is too difficult, it will not readily fit into the children's established schemata and they may feel frustrated.

A useful way to ensure that program content is adapted both to local conditions and the developmental level of children is to have small groups of parents discuss the ideas on which a program is based and alternative ways in which the ideas might be used and adapted to particular circumstances. Even more ideal would be for parents and teachers to meet periodically to discuss these and related ideas in order to work out more effective ways for school and home to encourage and support children.

Finally, even though our proposed program can be implemented without reference to other institutions, its implementation and impact are likely to be enhanced if it is embedded in and draws on the resources of other community agencies. Although the focus of the program is on the role of the family in supporting children's school learning, its locus of implementation (the home) is an institution embedded in other formal and nonformal social units and networks. Since many family units today lack the kinds of family and community support that would help them bring up their children, any efforts to harness community- and family-support networks for intervention programs are to be welcomed. Even if we regard the role of the family as being preeminent, we still have to recognize that other institutions and people in the community also have important roles to play in fostering children's educational development. Indeed, the more supportive links there are between the family and other contexts involving the child or persons responsible for his or her care, the greater will be the developmental potential of the family (Bronfenbrenner, 1979). The *Framework for Action* adopted at the World Conference on Education for All in Jomtien, Thailand, reminds us of this when it acknowledges the important role that community associations, cooperatives, religious bodies, and other nongovernmental organizations can play in providing and supporting basic education. In light of this acknowledgment, it is not surprising that the *Framework* goes on to stress the need to promote partnerships between such organizations through policies and mechanisms that strengthen their capacities and respect their autonomy (*World Declaration on Education for All and Framework for Action to Meet Basic Learning Needs*, 1990).

Initiating Home Intervention

On their own initiative, some parents may adopt ideas put forward in this book. For example, this may be true of parents who are financially comfortable but view child rearing as an impediment to the pursuit of their adult lives and are quite happy to see the school accept total responsibility for their children's education (see Redding, 1991). But for families not likely to come into contact with this or similar books, such a program will be initiated by an outside agency.

In many cases, parent education of the type outlined here, or any other kind of parent education for that matter, will be regarded as just one component in an array of services that might be provided for families (Powell, 1988). If the approach presented in this book is judged to meet the needs of particular families, there is no reason why it should not be included in a broader program encompassing a variety of measures designed to improve parental involvement in their children's education. In some situations, for example, it might be necessary to include education relating to health and nutrition (see Alvarez and Iriarte, 1991). Indeed, an early childhood intervention program or a parent involvement program can often provide a basis for penetration into a community leading to action in other areas, such as health provision (Chetley, 1990). Such programs might also be combined with more general efforts to improve communication between homes and schools, the establishment of school structures to accommodate the needs of parents and children, and the promotion of greater community involvement in family support and children's learning activities.

Although a variety of institutions can take the initiative in developing programs to support parents, the school is normally in the best position to do so. More than any other institution, it has access to families, it shares a relationship with them that is mutually beneficial to the mission of both, and it is in a position to secure parental participation in children's schooling and to continue to support that participation by coordinating, managing, supporting, and funding parental involvement (Epstein, 1987b; Henderson, Marburger, and Ooms, 1987; Nye, 1989; Walberg, 1984). Many schools already have structures in place designed to improve the schools' relationships with homes, structures that vary from parental representation on national agencies and on school councils to direct cooperation between teachers and parents in the classroom or in the home (see Wallace and Walberg, 1991). The type of program described in this book would obviously fit most readily into a structure that involved home-based activities. Further, it would seem particularly appropriate for parents who lack the self-confidence to become involved in school-based activities and so are likely to miss out on the advantages that accrue to their more confident peers who quickly respond to a school's invitation to participate in such activities (see Jones and Rowley, 1990).

A consideration of the problems that can arise in developing home-school links, as exemplified in a home program or in any other kind of arrangement, is beyond the scope of this book. However, we must at least acknowledge the existence of such problems, so as not to give the impression that parent involvement is always easily achieved. There is ample evidence that this is not so. A variety of explanations can be offered for this situation. Some parents do not appreciate that they have a key contribution to make to their children's education and leave education to the schools, feeling they have discharged their responsibilities when they send their children to school. Other parents may lack the confidence to approach schools. Schools too can create barriers to parents' involvement. They are not always parent-friendly, lacking flexibility and informality and thus making it difficult for parents to take the steps to greater involvement in school matters. Individual teachers, overprotective of their "professionalism," can also be an obstacle (Goldring, 1991), maintaining a position that is distant and autonomous from parents (Hulsebosch, 1991). And some teachers are naturally concerned about practical matters — the amount of time that might be involved in dealing with parents or their lack of preparation for the work (Goldring, 1991). Any one of these factors can alone or in combination with others give rise to mixed feelings in teachers about parent involvement, which exhibit themselves in ambivalence and tensions (Davies, 1991). At the same time, while such obstacles may at times be formidable, schools are likely to find rewarding any efforts they make to link home and school, not only in terms of improved student behavior and achievement but also in the support network that a close home-school partnership can provide for their work.

■ REFERENCES

Academic Development Institute. *Alliance for Achievement. Building the Value-Based School Community*. Chicago: Academic Development Institute, 1989.

Alan Guttmacher Institute. *Teenage Pregnancy: The Problem That Hasn't Gone Away*. New York: Alan Guttmacher Institute, 1981.

Alvarez, B., and Iriarte, N. *Familia y Aprendizaje. Lecciones de la Investigacion Reciente*. [Family and learning. Readings from recent research]. Ottawa, Canada: International Development Research Centre, 1991.

America 2000. An Education Strategy. Washington, D.C.: U.S. Department of Education, 1991.

Anastasi, A. "Intelligence and Family Size," *Psychological Bulletin*, 1956, *53*, 187–209.

Anderson, R. C., Wilson, P. T., and Fielding, L. G. "Growth in Reading and How Children Spend Their Time Outside of School," *Reading Research Quarterly*, 1988, *23*, 285–303.

Applebee, A. N., Langer, J. A., and Mullis, I.V.S. *Crossroads in American Education: The Nation's Report Card. A Summary of Findings*. Princeton, N.J.: Educational Testing Service, 1989.

Ariés, P. *Centuries of Childhood*. Harmondsworth, England: Penguin, 1973.

Aronowitz, S., and Giroux, H. A. "Schooling, Culture, and Literacy in the Age of Broken Dreams: A Review of Bloom and Hirsch," *Harvard Educational Review*, 1988, *58*, 172–194.

Atan, N. bt, Haji Abdullah, H. N. bt, Bakar Nordin, A., and Remot, S. b. "Remedial Reading Support Programme for Children in Grade 2 in Malaysia," *Evaluation in Education*, 1982, *6*, 137–160.

155

Baker, D. P., and Entwistle, D. R. "The Influence of Mothers on the Academic Expectations of Young Children: A Longitudinal Study of How Gender Differences Arise," *Social Forces,* 1987, *65,* 671–694.

Bali, S. K., Drenth, P.J.D., van der Flier, H., and Young, W. C. *Contribution of Aptitude Tests to the Prediction of School Performance in Kenya: A Longitudinal Study.* Lisse, Netherlands: Swets and Zeitlinger, 1984.

Barber, B. L., and Eccles, J. S. "Long-Term Influence of Divorce and Single-Parenting on Adolescent Family- and Work-Related Values, Behaviors, and Aspirations," *Psychological Bulletin,* 1992, *111,* 108–126.

Barker-Benfield, G. J. *The Cult of Sensibility.* Chicago: University of Chicago Press, 1992.

Barling, J. "Father's Employment: A Neglected Influence on Children." In J. V. Lerner and N. L. Galambos (eds.), *Employed Mothers and Their Children.* New York: Garland, 1991.

Bastiani, J. *Working with Parents. A Whole-School Approach.* Windsor, England: NFER-Nelson, 1989.

Bauch, J. P., Vietze, P. M., and Morris, V. D. "What Makes the Difference in Parental Participation?" *Childhood Education,* 1973, *59,* 47–54.

Baydar, N. E., and Brooks-Gunn, J. "Effects of Maternal Employment and Child-Care Arrangements on Preschoolers' Cognitive and Behavioral Outcomes: Evidence from the Children of the National Longitudinal Survey of Youth," *Developmental Psychology,* 1991, *27,* 932–945.

Becher, R. M. *Parent Involvement: A Review of Research and Principles of Effective Practice.* Washington, D.C.: National Institute of Health, 1984. (ED 247 032)

Becker, H. J., and Epstein, J. "Parent Involvement: A Survey of Teacher Practices," *Elementary School Journal,* 1982, *83,* 277–294.

Belmont, J. M. "Cognitive Strategies and Strategic Learning. The Socio-Instructional Approach," *American Psychologist,* 1989, *44,* 142–148.

Belmont, L., and Marolla, F. A. "Birth Order, Family Size, and Intelligence," *Science,* 1973, *182,* 1096–1101.

Belmont, L., Stein, S. A., and Susser, M. W. "Comparison of Associations of Birth Order with Intelligence Test Scores and Height," *Nature*, 1975, *255*, 54–56.

Bernstein, B. *Class, Codes and Control*. Vol. 1: *Theoretical Studies Towards a Sociology of Language*. London: Routledge & Kegan Paul, 1971.

Bernstein, B. (ed.). *Class, Codes and Control*. Vol. 2: *Applied Studies Towards a Sociology of Language*. London: Routledge & Kegan Paul, 1973.

Bernstein, B. *Class, Codes and Control*. Vol. 3: *Towards a Theory of Educational Transmissions*. London: Routledge & Kegan Paul, 1975.

Bloom, B. S. *Stability and Change in Human Characteristics*. New York: Wiley, 1964.

Bloom, B. S. "Implications of the IEA Studies for Curriculum and Instruction." In A. C. Purves and D. U. Levine (eds.), *Educational Policy and International Assessment*. Berkeley, Calif.: McCutchan, 1975.

Bloom, B. S. *Human Characteristics and School Learning*. New York: McGraw-Hill, 1976.

Bloom, B. S. *All Our Children Learning. A Primer for Parents, Teachers, and Other Educators*. New York: McGraw-Hill, 1981.

Bobbitt, N., and Paolucci, B. "Strengths of the Home and Family as Learning Environments." In R. J. Griffore and R. P. Boger (eds.), *Child Rearing in the Home and School*. New York: Plenum, 1986.

Bornstein, M. H. "Sensitive Periods in Development: Structural Characteristics and Causal Interpretations," *Psychological Bulletin*, 1989, *105*, 179–197.

Boulding, E. "Familia Faber: The Family as Maker of the Future," *Journal of Marriage and the Family*, 1983, *45*, 257–266.

Bradley, R., Caldwell, B. M., and Elardo, R. "Home Environment, Social Status, and Mental Test Performance," *Journal of Educational Psychology*, 1977, *69*, 697–701.

Bronfenbrenner, U. "Is Early Intervention Effective?" *Teachers College Record*, 1974, *76*, 279–303.

Bronfenbrenner, U. "Contexts of Childrearing. Problems and Prospects," *American Psychologist*, 1979, *34*, 844–850.

Bronfenbrenner, U. "Ecology of the Family as a Context for Human Development: Research Perspectives," *Developmental Psychology,* 1986, *22,* 723–742.

Bronfenbrenner, U., and Crouter, A. C. "Work and Family Through Time and Space." In S. B. Kamerman and C. D. Hayes (eds.), *Families That Work: Children in a Changing World.* Washington, D.C.: National Academy Press, 1982.

Brophy, J. E. "Mothers as Teachers of Their Own Preschool Children: The Influence of Socioeconomic Status and Task Structure on Teaching Specificity," *Child Development,* 1970, *41,* 79–94.

Brophy, J. E., and Good, T. L. *Teacher-Student Relationships: Causes and Consequences.* Troy, Mo.: Holt, Rinehart & Winston, 1974.

Brown, A. L., Bransford, J. D., Ferrara, R. A., and Campione, J. C. "Learning, Remembering, and Understanding." In P. H. Mussen (ed.), *Handbook of Child Psychology.* (4th ed.) Vol. 3: *Cognitive Development.* New York: Wiley, 1983.

Bruner, J. S. "The Cognitive Consequences of Early Sensory Deprivation." In P. Solomon and others (eds.), *Sensory Deprivation. A Symposium Held at Harvard Medical School.* Cambridge, Mass.: Harvard University Press, 1961.

Bruner, J. S. "Models of the Learner," *Educational Researcher,* 1985, *14*(6), 5–8.

Burks, B. S. "The Relative Influence of Nature and Nurture upon Mental Development: A Comparative Study of Foster Parent–Foster Child Resemblance and True Parent–True Child Resemblance." In L. M. Terman (chair), *Nature and Nurture: Their Influence upon Achievement. Twenty-Seventh Yearbook of the National Society for the Study of Education, Part II.* Chicago: National Society for the Study of Education, 1928.

Burt, C. *Intelligence and Fertility.* London: Eugenics Society, 1946.

Caplan, N., Choy, M. H., and Whitmore, J. K. "Indochinese Refugee Families and Academic Achievement," *Scientific American,* 1992, *266*(2), 36–42.

CENECA, FLASCO. (Centro de Communicación y Cultura para El Desarrollo, Faculdad Latina Américana de Estudios Sociales). *Encuesta consumo popular* [Consumer behavior survey]. Santiago, Chile: Author, 1987.

Chase-Landsdale, P. L., Michael, R. T., and Desai, S. "Maternal Employment During Infancy: An Analysis of Children of the National Longitudinal Survey of Youth (NLSY)." In J. V. Lerner and N. L. Galambos (eds.), *Employed Mothers and Their Children*. New York: Garland, 1991.

Cherlin, A. *Marriage, Divorce, Remarriage*. Cambridge, Mass.: Harvard University Press, 1981.

Chetley, A. *The Power to Change. The Experience of the Costa Atlántica Project in Colombia (1977–1989)*. The Hague: van Leer Foundation, 1990.

Chrispeels, J. H. "District Leadership in Parent Involvement. Policies and Actions in San Diego," *Phi Delta Kappan*, 1991, *72*, 367–371.

Cicirelli, V. G. "The Relationship of Sibling Structure to Intellectual Abilities and Achievement," *Review of Educational Research*, 1978, *48*, 365–379.

Clarke-Stewart, K. A., and Apfel, N. "Evaluating Parental Effects on Child Development," *Review of Research in Education*, 1978, *6*, 47–119.

Cochran, M. "Parental Empowerment in Family Matters: Lessons Learned from a Research Program." In D. R. Powell (ed.), *Parent Education as Early Childhood Intervention: Emerging Directions in Theory, Research and Practice*. Vol. 3: *Annual Advances in Applied Developmental Psychology*. Norwood, N.J.: Ablex, 1988.

Cochran, M., and Dean, C. "Home-School Relations and the Empowerment Process," *Elementary School Journal*, 1991, *91*, 261–270.

Cochran, M., and Woolever, F. "Beyond the Deficit Model: The Empowerment of Parents with Information and Informal Supports." In I. E. Sigel and L. M. Laosa (eds.), *Changing Families*. New York: Plenum, 1983.

Coleman, J. S. "Families and Schools," *Educational Researcher*, 1987, *16*(6), 32–38.

Coleman, J. S. *Foundations of Social Theory*. Cambridge, Mass.: Harvard University Press, 1990.

Coleman, J. S., and Husén, T. *Becoming Adult in a Changing Society*. Paris: Organisation for Economic Cooperation and Development, 1985.

Coleman, J. S., and others. *Equality of Educational Opportunity.* Washington, D.C.: Office of Education, U.S. Department of Health, Education and Welfare, 1966.

Comer, J. P. "Home-School Relationships as They Affect the Academic Success of Children," *Education and Urban Society,* 1984, *16,* 323–337.

Comer, J. P. "Educating Poor Minority Children," *Scientific American,* 1988, *259*(5), 42–48.

Cummings, W. K. "Evaluation and Examinations." In R. M. Thomas (ed.), *International Comparative Education. Practices, Issues, and Prospects.* New York: Pergamon Press, 1990.

D'Angelo, D. A., and Adler, C. R. "Chapter 1: A Catalyst for Improving Parent Involvement," *Phi Delta Kappan,* 1991, *72,* 350–354.

Davé, R. H. "The Identification and Measurement of Environmental Process Variables That Are Related to Educational Achievement." Unpublished doctoral dissertation, University of Chicago, 1963.

Davidson, J. L., Lia, D., and Troyer, C. R. "Emerging Literacy: What We Know Should Determine What We Do." In J. L. Davidson (ed.), *Counterpoint and Beyond. A Response to Becoming a Nation of Readers.* Urbana, Ill.: National Council of Teachers of English, 1988.

Davies, D. "Schools Reaching Out. Family, School, and Community Partnerships for Student Success," *Phi Delta Kappan,* 1991, *72,* 376–382.

Dolan, L. J. "The Affective Correlates of Home Concern and Support, Instructional Quality, and Achievement." Unpublished doctoral dissertation, University of Chicago, 1980.

Dolan, L. J. "Home, School and Pupil Attitudes," *Evaluation in Education,* 1981, *4,* 265–358.

Dornbush, S. *Helping Your Kid Make the Grade.* Reston, Va.: National Association of Secondary School Principals, 1986.

Dorr, A. *Television and Children. A Special Medium for a Special Audience.* Newbury Park, Calif.: Sage, 1986.

Douglas, J.W.B. *The Home and the School. A Study of Ability and Attainment in Primary School.* London: MacGibbon and Kee, 1964.

Dreeben, R. *On What Is Learned in School.* Reading, Mass.: Addison-Wesley, 1968.

Drenth, P.J.D., van der Flier, H., and Omari, I. M. "Educational Selection in Tanzania," *Evaluation in Education,* 1983, *7,* 95–209.

Duvall, E. M. "Conceptions of Parenthood," *American Journal of Sociology,* 1946, *52,* 193–203.

Dyer, D. P. "The Effects of Environmental Variables on the Achievement of Elementary School Children in Trinidad." Unpublished doctoral dissertation, University of Alberta, 1967.

Eells, K., and others. *Intelligence and Cultural Differences.* Chicago: University of Chicago Press, 1951.

Elley, W. B. *How in the World Do Students Read? IEA Study of Reading Literacy.* The Hague: International Association for the Evaluation of Educational Achievement, 1992.

Epstein, J. L. "Parents' Reactions to Teacher Practices in Parent Involvement," *Elementary School Journal,* 1986, *56,* 277–294.

Epstein, J. L. "Parent Involvement: What the Research Says to Administrators," *Education and Urban Society,* 1987a, *19,* 119–136.

Epstein, J. L. "What Principals Should Know About Parent Involvement," *Principal,* 1987b, *66*(3), 6–9.

Epstein, J. L. "Effects on Student Achievement of Teachers' Practices of Parent Involvement." In S. Silvern (ed.), *Literacy Through Family, Community, and School Interaction.* Vol. 5: *Advances in Reading/Language Research.* Greenwich, Conn.: JAI, 1991a.

Epstein, J. L. "Paths to Partnership: What We Can Learn From Federal, State, District, and School Initiatives," *Phi Delta Kappan,* 1991b, *72,* 344–349.

Erickson, E. H. *Childhood and Society.* New York: W. W. Norton, 1950.

Fine, M. J. (ed.). *Handbook on Parent Education.* San Diego, Calif.: Academic Press, 1980.

Fine, M. J. (ed.). *The Second Handbook on Parent Education, Contemporary Perspectives.* San Diego, Calif: Academic Press, 1989.

Fitzgerald, M. I. *A Study of the Relationship Between Home Achieve-*

ment and Certain Home Process Variables. Unpublished master's thesis, National University of Ireland, 1975.

Florin, P. R., and Dokecki, P. R. "Changing Families Through Parent and Family Education: Review and Analysis." In I. E. Sigel and L. M. Laosa (eds.), *Changing Families.* New York: Plenum, 1983.

Floud, J., Halsey, A. H., and Martin, F. M. *Social Class and Educational Opportunity.* London: Heinemann, 1957.

Fraser, E. *Home Environment and the School.* London: University of London Press, 1959.

Galambos, N. L., and Maggs, J. L. "Children in Self-Care: Figures, Facts, and Fiction." In J. V. Lerner and N. L. Galambos (eds.), *Employed Mothers and Their Children.* New York: Garland, 1991.

Gay, J., and Cole, M. *The New Mathematics and an Old Culture: A Study of Learning Among the Kpelle of Liberia.* Troy, Mo.: Holt, Rinehart & Winston, 1967.

Giaquinta, J., and Ely, M. *A Longitudinal Study of Children's Educational Microcomputing at Home.* New York: Project Site, New York University, 1986.

Gillum, R. M. "The Effects of Parent Involvement on Student Achievement in Three Michigan Performance Contracting Programs." Paper presented at the annual meeting of the American Educational Research Association, New York, April 1977.

Glaser, R. "Learning Theory and Theories of Knowledge." In E. De Corte, H. Lodewijks, R. Parmentier, and P. Span (eds.), *Learning and Instruction.* New York: Pergamon Press, 1987.

Goldring, E. B. "Parents: Participants in an Organizational Framework," *International Journal of Educational Research,* 1991, *15*, 215–228.

Good, T. L. "What Is Learned in Elementary Schools." In T. M. Tomlinson and H. J. Walberg (eds.), *Academic Work and Educational Excellence.* Berkeley, Calif.: McCutchan, 1986.

Goodson, B., and Hess, R. *Effects of Parent Training Programs on Child Performance and Parent Behaviors.* Chapel Hill: University of North Carolina, 1976. (ED 136 912)

Gordon, I. J. *An Early Intervention Project: A Longitudinal Look.* Gainesville, Fla.: Institute for Development of Human Resources, 1973.

Gordon, I. J., Olmsted, P., Robin, R., and True, J. "How Has Follow Through Promoted Parent Involvement?" *Young Children,* 1979, *34,* 49–53.

Gottfried, A. E., and Gottfried, A. W. *Maternal Employment and Children's Development. Longitudinal Research.* New York: Plenum, 1988.

Gotts, E. E. "Long-Term Effects of a Home-Oriented Preschool Program," *Childhood Education,* 1980, *56,* 228–234.

Gouke, M. N., and Rollins, A. M. *One-Parent Children, The Growing Minority. A Research Guide.* New York: Garland, 1990.

Graue, N. E., Weinstein, T., and Walberg, H. J. "School-Based Home Instruction and Learning: A Quantitative Synthesis," *Journal of Educational Research,* 1983, *76,* 351–360.

Gray, S. W, and Klaus, R. A. "The Early Training Project: A Seventh-Year Report," *Child Development,* 1970, *41,* 909–924.

Gray, S. W., and Wandersman, L. P. "The Methodology of Home-Based Intervention Studies: Problems and Promising Strategies," *Child Development,* 1980, *51,* 993–1009.

Greaney, V. "Factors Related to Amount and Type of Leisure Time Reading," *Reading Research Quarterly,* 1980, *15,* 337–357.

Greaney, V., and Hegarty, M. "Correlates of Leisure Time Reading," *Journal of Research in Reading,* 1987, *10,* 3–20.

Greaney, V., and Kellaghan, T. *Equality of Opportunity in Irish Schools.* Dublin: Educational Company, 1984.

Great Britain: Department of Education and Science. *Children and Their Primary Schools.* 2 vols. London: Her Majesty's Stationery Office, 1967.

Griffore, R. J., and Bubolz, M. "Limits and Possibilities of Family and School as Educators." In R. J. Griffore and R. P. Boger (eds.), *Child Rearing in the Home and the School.* New York: Plenum, 1986.

Gross, M. "Combined Human Efforts in Elevating Achievement at the Wheatly School, Washington, DC." Ed.D. practicum, Nova University, Fort Lauderdale, Fla., 1974.

Guinagh, B., and Gordon, I. J. *School Performance as a Function of Early Stimulation.* Gainesville, Fla.: Institute for Development of Human Resources, University of Florida, 1976.

Halpern, R. "Effects of Early Childhood Intervention on Primary School Progress in Latin America," *Comparative Education Review,* 1986, *30,* 193–215.

Halpern, R., and Myers, R. *Effects of Early Childhood Intervention on Primary School Progress and Performance in the Developing Countries.* Ypsilanti, Mich.: High Scope Eductional Research Foundation, 1985.

Hannon, P. "A Study of the Effects of Parent Involvement in Teaching of Reading on Children's Reading Test Performance," *British Journal of Educational Psychology,* 1987, *57,* 56–72.

Hanson, R. A. "Consistency and Stability of Home Environmental Measures Related to IQ," *Child Development,* 1975, *46,* 470–480.

Harter, S. "Developmental Perspectives on the Self-Systems." In P. H. Mussen (ed.), *Handbook of Child Psychology.* (4th ed.) Vol. 4: *Socialization, Personality, and Social Development.* New York: Wiley, 1983.

Hebb, D. O. *The Organization of Behavior.* New York: Wiley, 1949.

Heer, D. M. "Effects of Sibling Number on Child Outcome," *Annual Review of Sociology,* 1985, *11,* 27–47.

Henderson, A. T. (ed.). *Parent Participation–Student Achievement: The Evidence Grows.* Columbia, Md.: National Committee for Citizens in Education, 1981.

Henderson, A. T. (ed.). *The Evidence Continues to Grow: Parent Involvement Improves Student Achievement.* Washington, D.C.: National Committee for Citizens in Education, 1984.

Henderson, A. T., Marburger, C. L., and Ooms, T. "Building a Family-School Relationship," *Principal,* 1987, *66*(3), 12–13.

Henderson, R. W. "Home Environment and Intellectual Performance." In R. W. Henderson (ed.), *Parent-Child Interaction.* New York: Academic Press, 1981.

Herman, J. L., and Yeh, J. P. "Some Effects of Parent Involvement in the Schools," *Urban Review,* 1983, *15*(1), 11–17.

Hess, R. D. "Approaches to the Measurement and Interpretation of Parent-Child Interaction." In R. W. Henderson (ed.), *Parent-Child Interaction.* New York: Academic Press, 1981.

Hess, R. D., and Azuma, H. "Cultural Support for Schooling. Contrasts Between Japan and the United States," *Educational Researcher,* 1991, *20*(9), 2–8.

Hess, R. D., and Holloway, S. D. "Family and School as Educational Institutions," *Review of Child Development Research,* 1984, *7,* 179–217.

Hess, R. D., and Shipman, V. C. "Early Experience and the Socialization of Cognitive Modes in Children," *Child Development,* 1965, *36,* 869–886.

Hess, R. D., and Shipman, V. C. "Cognitive Elements in Maternal Behavior." In J. P. Hill (ed.), *Minnesota Symposia on Child Psychology.* Vol. 1. Minneapolis: University of Minnesota Press, 1967.

Hewison, J. "The Long-Term Effectiveness of Parental Involvement in Reading: A Follow-Up of the Haringey Project," *British Journal of Educational Psychology,* 1988, *58,* 184–190.

Heyneman, S. P., and Loxley, W. "The Effect of Primary School Quality on Achievement Across Twenty-Nine High- and Low-Income Countries," *American Journal of Sociology,* 1983, *88,* 1162–1194.

Hodgkinson, H. "Reform Versus Reality," *Phi Delta Kappan,* 1991, *73,* 9–16.

Hoffer, T. B., and Coleman, J. S. "Changing Families and Communities: Implications for Schools." In B. Mitchell and L. L. Cunningham (eds.), *Educational Leadership and Changing Contexts of Families, Communities, and Schools. Eighty-Ninth Yearbook of the National Society for the Study of Education, Part II.* Chicago: National Society for the Study of Education, 1990.

Houston, S. H. "A Reexamination of Some Assumptions About the Language of the Disadvantaged Child," *Child Development,* 1970, *41,* 947–963.

Hulsebosch, P. L. "Beauty in the Eye of the Beholder: How and Why Teachers Involve Parents," *International Journal of Educational Research,* 1991, *15,* 183–200.

Hunt, J. McV. *Intelligence and Experience.* New York: Ronald Press, 1961.

Hunt, J. McV. "Psychological Development: Early Experience," *Annual Review of Psychology,* 1979, *30,* 103–143.

Hymas, C. "Black Pupils Beat Whites in Classroom Tests." London *Sunday Times,* 12 January, 1992, p. 3.

International Labour Office. *Year Book of Labour Statistics.* (45th issue.) Geneva: International Labour Office, 1985.

Irvine, D. J. *Parent Involvement Affects Children's Cognitive Growth.* Albany: State Education Department, Division of Research, University of the State of New York, 1979. (ED 176 893)

Irwin, M. H., Schafer, G. N., and Feiden, C. P. "Emic and Unfamiliar Category Sorting of Mano Farmers and U.S. Undergraduates," *Journal of Cross-Cultural Psychology,* 1974, *5,* 407–423.

Iverson, B. K., and Walberg, H. J. "Home Environment and School Learning: A Quantitative Synthesis," *Journal of Experimental Education,* 1982, *50*(3), 144–151.

Jackson, P. W. *Life in Classrooms.* Troy, Mo.: Holt, Rinehart & Winston, 1968.

Janhom, S. "Educating Parents to Educate Their Children." Unpublished doctoral dissertation, University of Chicago, 1983.

Johnstone, J. N., and Jiyono. "Out-of-School Factors and Educational Achievement in Indonesia," *Comparative Education Review,* 1983, *27,* 278–295.

Jolly, R., and Cornia, A. *Efectos de la recesión mundial sobre la infancia.* [Effects of the world recession on childhood]. Madrid: Siglo XXI de Espana Editores, 1984.

Jones, M., and Rowley, G. "What Does Research Say About Parental Participation in Children's Reading Development?" *Evaluation and Research in Education,* 1990, *4,* 21–36.

Joseph, P. B. "The Changing American Family," *Social Education,* 1986, *50,* 458–463.

Kagan, J. "Family Experience and the Child's Development," *American Psychologist,* 1979, *34,* 886–891.

Kahl, J. A., and Davis, J. A. "A Comparison of Indexes of Socioeconomic Status," *American Sociological Review,* 1955, *20,* 317–325.

Kalinowski, A., and Sloane, K. "The Home Environment and

School Achievement," *Studies in Educational Evaluation*, 1981, *7*, 85–96.

Karen, M. "The Effects of Industrialization on Men's Attitudes Toward the Extended Family and Women's Rights: A Cross-National Study," *Journal of Marriage and the Family*, 1984, *46*, 153–160.

Keeves, J. P. *Educational Environment and Student Attainment*. Stockholm: Almquist and Wiksell, 1972.

Keeves, J. P. "Educational Environment and Student Achievement." In K. Marjoribanks (ed.), *Environments for Learning*. Windsor, England: NFER Publishing, 1974.

Keeves, J. P. "The Home, the School, and Achievement in Mathematics and Science," *Science Education*, 1975, *59*, 439–460.

Kellaghan, T. "Abstraction and Categorization in African Children," *International Journal of Psychology*, 1968, *3*, 115–120.

Kellaghan, T. "Relationships Between Home Environment and Scholastic Behavior in a Disadvantaged Population," *Journal of Educational Psychology*, 1977a, *69*, 754–760.

Kellaghan, T. *The Evaluation of an Intervention Programme for Disadvantaged Children*. Windsor, England: NFER Publishing, 1977b.

Kellaghan, T., and Macnamara, J. "Family Correlates of Verbal Reasoning Ability," *Developmental Psychology*, 1972, *7*, 49–53.

Kessen, W., and Fein, G. *Variations in Home-Based Infant Education: Language, Play, and Social Development. Final Report*. Washington, D.C.: Office of Child Development, 1975. (ED 118 233)

Kifer, E. "Relationships Between Academic Achievement and Personality Characteristics: A Quasi-Longitudinal Study," *American Educational Research Journal*, 1975, *12*, 191–210.

Kohn, M. L. "Social Class and Parent-Child Relationships: An Interpretation," *American Journal of Sociology*, 1963, *68*, 471–480.

Kondakov, M. I. "The Road to Educational Reform in the USSR," *Perspectives*, 1987, *17*, 27–35.

Kontos, S. "The Role of Continuity and Context in Children's Relationships with Nonparental Adults." In R. C. Pianta (ed.), *Beyond the Parent: The Role of Other Adults in Children's Lives.* New Directions for Child Development, no. 57. San Francisco: Jossey-Bass, 1992.

Laboratory of Comparative Human Cognition. "Culture and Cognitive Development." In P. H. Mussen (ed.), *Handbook of Child Psychology.* (4th ed.) Vol. 1: *History, Theory, and Methods.* New York: Wiley, 1983.

Labov, W. *Language in the Inner City.* Philadelphia: University of Pennsylvania Press, 1972.

Landers, C., and Myers, R. "Home-Based Programmes for Early Childhood Care and Development. Part II: Educating Parents and Other Caregivers," *Coordinator's Notebook,* 1988, *5,* 2–9.

Laosa, L. M. "School, Occupation, Culture and Family: The Impact of Parental Schooling on the Parent-Child Relationship," *Journal of Educational Psychology,* 1982, *74,* 791–827.

Lapointe, A. E., Mead, N. A., and Phillips, G. W. *A World of Differences. An International Assessment of Mathematics and Science.* Princeton, N.J.: Educational Testing Service, 1988.

Lasater, T. M., Malone, P., and Ferguson, C. *Birmingham Parent-Child Development Center. Final Report.* Birmingham, Ala.: Parent-Child Development Center, 1976. (ED 211 236)

Lavin, D. E. *The Prediction of Academic Performance.* New York: Russell Sage Foundation, 1965.

Lazar, I., and others. *The Persistence of Preschool Effects. A Long-Term Follow-up of Fourteen Infants and Preschool Experiments.* Publication No. (OHDS) 78–30129. Washington, D.C.: U.S. Government Printing Office, 1977.

Lefcourt, H. M. *Locus of Control: Current Trends in Theory and Research.* New York: Halstead, 1976.

Leler, H. "Parent Education and Involvement in Relation to the Schools and to Parents of School-Aged Children." In R. Haskins and J. J. Gallagher (eds.), *Parent Education and Public Policy.* Norwood, N.J.: Ablex, 1983.

Leler, H., and others. *Houston Parent-Child Development Center. Progress Report.* Houston, Tex.: University of Houston, 1975.

Lerner, J. V., and Galambos, N. L. "Employed Mothers and Their Children: A View of the Issues." In J. V. Lerner and

N. L. Galambos (eds.), *Employed Mothers and Their Children*. New York: Garland, 1991.

Lesser, G., Fifer, G., and Clark, D. "Mental Abilities of Children from Different Social-Class and Cultural Groups," *Monographs of the Society for Research in Child Development*, 1965, *30*(4, Serial No. 102).

Levenson, H. "Differentiating Among Internality, Powerful Others, and Change." In H. M. Lefcourt (ed.), *Research with the Locus of Control Construct*. Vol 1: *Assessment Methods*. New York: Academic Press, 1981.

Levenstein, P. "Cognitive Growth in Preschoolers Through Verbal Interactions with Mothers," *American Journal of Orthopsychiatry*, 1970, *40*, 426–432.

Linnan, R. J. "Ethnic Comparisons of Environmental Predictors of Three Cognitive Abilities." Unpublished doctoral dissertation, Boston College, 1976.

Lockheed, M. E., and Verspoor, A. M. *Improving Primary Education in Developing Countries*. Oxford, England: Oxord University Press, 1991.

Love, J. M., and others. *Home Start Evaluation Study*. Cambridge, Mass.: Abt Associates, 1976.

Lozoff, B. "Nutrition and Behavior," *American Psychologist*, 1989, *44*, 231–236.

Lull, J. "The Social Uses of Television," *Human Communications Research*, 1980, *6*, 197–209.

Luscher, K. "Knowledge on Socialization." Paper presented at the Cornell University Conference on Research Perspectives in the Ecology of Human Development, Ithaca, N.Y., 1977.

McGillicuddy-DeLisi, A. V. "The Relationship Between Parents' Beliefs About Development and Family Constellation, Socioeconomic Status, and Parents' Teaching Strategies." In L. M. Laosa and I. E. Sigel (eds.), *Families as Learning Environments for Children*. New York: Plenum, 1982.

McGurk, L. J. "A Study of the Relationships Between the Educational Environment of the Home and Student Achievement at Two Different Grade Levels." Unpublished doctoral dissertation, Boston College, 1973.

MacLeod, F. "Parental Involvement in Education: The Coventry Experience," *Early Child Development and Care*, 1985, *21*, 83–90.

MacPhee, D., Ramey, C. T., and Yeates, K. O. "Home Environment and Early Cognitive Development: Implications for Intervention." In A. W. Gottfried (ed.), *Home Environment and Early Cognitive Development, Longitudinal Research*. New York: Academic Press, 1984.

Madaus, G. F., Airasian, P. W., and Kellaghan, T. *School Effectiveness. A Reassessment of the Evidence*. New York: McGraw-Hill, 1980.

Marjoribanks, K. "Academic Achievement: Family Size and Social Class Correlates." In K. Marjoribanks (ed.), *Environments for Learning*. Windsor, England: NFER Publishing, 1974a.

Marjoribanks, K. "Environmental Correlates of Abilities: A Canonical Analysis." In K. Marjoribanks (ed.), *Environments for Learning*. Windsor, England: NFER Publishing, 1974b.

Marjoribanks, K. "Sibsize, Family Environment, Cognitive Performance, and Affective Characteristics," *Journal of Psychology*, 1976, *94*, 195–204.

Marjoribanks, K. "Family and School Environmental Correlates of School-Related Affective Characteristics: An Australian Study," *Journal of Social Psychology*, 1978, *106*, 181–189.

Marjoribanks, K. *Families and Their Learning Environments. An Empirical Analysis*. London: Routledge & Kegan Paul, 1979a.

Marjoribanks, K. "Family Environments." In H. J. Walberg (ed.), *Educational Environments and Effects*. Berkeley, Calif.: McCutchan, 1979b.

Marjoribanks, K. "Ability and Attitude Correlates of Academic Achievement: Family Group Differences," *Journal of Educational Psychology*, 1987, *79*, 171–178.

Marjoribanks, K., Walberg, H. J., and Bargen, M. "Mental Abilities: Sibling Constellation and Social Class Correlates," *British Journal of Social and Clinical Psychology*, 1975, *14*, 109–116.

Martin, L., and Culter, S. "Mortality Decline and Japanese Family Structure," *Population and Development Review*, 1983, *9*, 633–650.

Martin, M. O. "Reading and Socioeconomic Background: A Progressive Achievement Gap?" *Irish Journal of Education,* 1979, *13,* 62–78.

Mayer, S. E., and Jencks, C. "Growing Up in Poor Neighborhoods: How Much Does It Matter?" *Science,* 1989, *243,* 1441–1445.

Moles, O. "Synthesis of Recent Research on Parent Participation in Children's Education," *Educational Leadership,* 1982, *40*(1), 44–47.

Moll, L. C., and Diaz, S. "Change as the Goal of Educational Research," *Anthropology and Education Quarterly,* 1987, *18,* 300–311.

Myers, R. "Effects of Early Childhood Intervention on Primary School Progress and Performance in the Developing Countries." Paper presented at seminar on the Importance of Nutrition and Early Stimulation for the Education of Children in the Third World. Stockholm, April 6–9, 1988. Ypsilanti, Mich.: High/Scope Educational Research Foundation, 1988.

National Commission on Excellence in Education. *A Nation at Risk. The Imperative for Educational Reform.* Washington, D.C.: U.S. Government Printing Office, 1983.

Nisbet, J. D., and Entwistle, N. J. "Intelligence and Family Size, 1949–1965," *British Journal of Educational Psychology,* 1967, *37,* 188–193.

Nye, B. A. "Effective Parent Education and Involvement Models and Programs: Contemporary Strategies for School Implementation." In M. J. Fine (ed.), *The Second Handbook on Parent Education, Contemporary Perspectives.* New York: Academic Press, 1989.

Oakes, J., and Lipton, M. *Making the Best of Schools. A Handbook for Parents, Teachers, and Policymakers.* New Haven, Conn.: Yale University Press, 1990.

Ogbu, J. U. "Cultural Discontinuities and Schooling," *Anthropology and Education Quarterly,* 1982, *13,* 290–307.

Ogbu, J. U. "Variability in Minority School Performance: A Problem in Search of an Explanation," *Anthropology and Education Quarterly,* 1987, *18,* 312–334.

Ogbu, J. U. "Immigrant and Involuntary Minorities in Comparative Perspective." In M. A. Gibson and J. U. Ogbu (eds.), *Minority Status and Schooling. A Comparative Study of Immigrant and Involuntary Minorities.* New York: Garland, 1991.

Olmsted, P. P. "Parent Involvement in Elementary Education: Findings and Suggestions from the Follow-Through Program," *Elementary School Journal,* 1991, *91,* 221–231.

Olmsted, P. P., and Jester, R. E. "Mother-Child Interaction in a Teaching Situation," *Theory into Practice,* 1972, *11,* 163–170.

Olmsted, P. P., and Rubin, R. "Linking Parent Behaviors to Child Achievement: Four Evaluation Studies from the Parent Education Follow-Through Program," *Studies in Educational Evaluation,* 1982, *8,* 317–325.

Omari, I. M., and others. *Universal Primary School in Tanzania.* Ottawa, Canada: International Development Research Centre, 1983.

Ostlund, K., Gennaro, E., and Dobbert, M. "A Naturalistic Study of Children and Their Parents in Family Learning Courses in Science," *Journal of Research in Science Teaching,* 1985, *22,* 723–741.

Owen, T. E. *The Consequences of Schooling: A Review of Research on the Outcomes of Primary Schooling in Developing Countries.* Education Development Discussion Paper, No. 3. Montreal, Canada: Center for Cognitive and Ethnographic Studies, McGill University, 1988.

Pallas, A. M., Natriello, G., and McDill, E. L. "The Changing Nature of the Disadvantaged Population. Current Dimensions and Future Trends," *Educational Researcher,* 1989, *18*(5), 16–22.

Palmer, F. H. "The Effects of Early Childhood Intervention." Paper presented at the annual meeting of the American Association for the Advancement of Science, Denver, Colo., 1977.

Papagiannis, G. J., Douglas, C., Williamson, N., and Le Mon, R. *Information Technology and Education. Implications for Theory, Research and Practice.* Manuscript Report MR161e. Ottawa, Canada: International Development Research Centre, 1987.

Passow, A. H. *Deprivation and Disadvantage. Nature and Manifesta-*

tions. Hamburg, Germany: UNESCO Institute for Education, 1970.

Paz, R. *Paths to Empowerment. Ten Years of Early Childhood Work in Israel.* The Hague: van Leer Foundation, 1990.

Perkins, D. N., and Solomon, G. "Are Cognitive Skills Context-Bound?" *Educational Researcher,* 1989, *18*(1), 16–25.

Peters, D. L., Bollin, G. G., and Murphy, R. E. "Head Start's Influence on Parental Competence and Child Competence." In S. Silvern (ed.), *Literacy Through Family, Community, and School Interaction. Advances in Reading/Language Research.* Vol. 5. Greenwich, Conn.: JAI Press, 1991.

Peterson, R. A. "Revitalizing the Culture Concept." *Annual Review of Sociology,* 1979, *5,* 137–166.

Philips, S. U. "Commentary: Access to Power and Maintenance of Ethnic Identity as Goals of Multi-Cultural Education," *Anthropology and Education Quarterly,* 1976, *7*(4), 30–32.

Piaget, J. *The Psychology of Intelligence.* London: Routledge & Kegan Paul, 1950.

Pollitt, E. *Malnutrition and Infection in the Classroom.* Paris: UNESCO, 1990.

Powell, D. R. "Correlates of Parent-Teacher Communication Frequency and Diversity," *Journal of Educational Research,* 1978, *71,* 333–341.

Powell, D. R. "Individual Differences in Participation in Parent-Child Support Programs." In I. E. Sigel and L. M. Laosa (eds.), *Changing Families.* New York: Plenum, 1983.

Powell, D. R. "Parent Education and Support Programs," *Young Children,* 1986, *41*(3), 47–53.

Powell, D. R. "Emerging Directions in Parent-Child Early Intervention." In D. R. Powell (ed.), *Parent Education as Early Childhood Intervention: Emerging Directions in Theory, Research and Practice.* Vol. 3: *Annual Advances in Applied Development Psychology.* Norwood, N.J.: Ablex, 1988.

Preston, S. M. "Children and the Elderly in the U.S." *Scientific American,* 1984, *251*(6), 36–41.

Pugh, G., and De'Ath, E. *Working Towards Partnership in the Early Years.* London: National Children's Bureau, 1989.

Raczynski, D. *Disminuyó la Extrema Pobreza Entre 1970 y 1982?*

[Did extreme poverty decrease between 1970 and 1982?] Notas Tecnicas no. 90. Santiago, Chile: Corporación de Investigaciones Económicas para América Latina, 1986.

Radin, N. "The Impact of a Kindergarten Home Counseling Program," *Exceptional Children*, 1969, *36*, 251–256.

Radin, N. "Three Degrees of Maternal Involvement in a Preschool Program: Impact on Mothers and Children," *Child Development*, 1972, *43*, 1355–1364.

Ramirez, A. E. "Where Have All the Children Gone?" *IRDC Reports*, 1987, *16*(1), 22–23.

Rankin, R. "Methodology in Environmental Research." In R. W. Henderson (ed.), *Parent-Child Intervention*. New York: Academic Press, 1981.

Rappaport, J. "In Praise of Paradox: A Social Policy of Empowerment Over Prevention," *American Journal of Community Psychology*, 1981, *9*, 1–25.

Redding, S. "Alliance for Achievement: An Action Plan for Educators and Parents," *International Journal of Educational Research*, 1991, *15*, 147–162.

Rich, D. *The Forgotten Factor in School Success: The Family*. Washington, D.C.: Home and School Institute, 1985.

Rich, D. *Schools and Families: Issues and Actions*. Washington, D.C.: Home and School Institute, 1987.

Richards, M. H., and Duckett, E. "Maternal Employment and Adolescence." In J. V. Lerner and N. L. Galambos (eds.), *Employed Mothers and Their Children*. New York: Garland, 1991.

Ritter, P. L., and Dornbusch, S. M. "Ethnic Variation in Family Influences on Academic Achievement." Paper presented at a meeting of the American Educational Research Association, San Francisco, March 1989.

Rohwer, W. D. "Learning, Race, and School Success," *Review of Educational Research*, 1971, *41*, 191–210.

Rosenberg, B. Q., and Sutton-Smith, B. "Sibling Age Spacing Effects Upon Cognition," *Developmental Psychology*, 1969, *1*, 661–663.

Rutter, M. "Family and School Influences on Behavioural Development," *Journal of Child Psychology and Psychiatry*, 1985a, *26*, 349–368.

Rutter, M. "Family and School Influences on Cognitive Development," *Journal of Child Psychology and Psychiatry,* 1985b, *26,* 683-704.

Ryan, S. "Home-School-Community Liaison: The Irish Experience." Paper presented at the 4th annual International Roundtable on Families, Communities, Schools, and Children's Learning, San Francisco, April 1992.

Sattes, B. D. *Parent Involvement: A Review of the Literature.* AEL Occasional paper no. 021. Charleston, W. Va.: Appalachia Educational Laboratory, 1985.

Schaefer, E. "Parents as Educators: Evidence from Cross-Sectional, Longitudinal, and Intervention Research," *Young Children,* 1972, *28,* 227-239.

Schiefelbein, E., and Simons, J. *Los determinantes del rendimiento escolar: Reseña de la investigación para los paises en desarrollo.* [The determinants of school achievement: Review of the research for developing countries]. Bogotá, Columbia: Centro Internacional de Investigaciones para el Desarrollo, 1981.

Schleicher, K. "Home-School Relations and Parental Participation." In M. Galton and A. Blyth (eds.), *Handbook of Primary Education in Europe.* London: David Fulton, 1989.

Schlossman, S. "Before Home Start: Notes Toward a History of Parent Education in America," *Harvard Educational Review,* 1976, *46,* 436-467.

Scott-Jones, D. "Family Influences on Cognitive Development and School Achievement," *Review of Research in Education,* 1984, *11,*259-304.

Sears, P. S., and Dowley, E. M. "Research on Teaching in the Nursery School." In N. L. Gage (ed.), *Handbook of Research on Teaching.* Chicago: Rand McNally, 1963.

Shavelson, R. J., Hubner, J. J., and Stanton, G. C. "Self-Concept: Validation of Construct Interpretations," *Review of Educational Research,* 1976, *46,* 407-441.

Sigel, I. E., and Laosa, L. M. (eds.). *Changing Families.* New York: Plenum, 1983.

Silvern, S. "Parent Involvement and Reading Achievement: A Review of Research and Implications for Practice," *Childhood Education,* 1985, *62*(1), 44-49.

Silvern, S. "Continuity/Discontinuity Between Home and Early Childhood Education Environments," *Elementary School Journal*, 1988, *89*, 147–160.

Simitis, S. "Children's Rights in European Countries." In V. Greaney (ed.), *Children: Needs and Rights*. New York: Irvington, 1985.

Siu, S-F. *Towards an Understanding of Chinese-American Educational Achievement. A Literature Review*. Boston: Center on Families, Communities, Schools and Children's Learning, 1992.

Slaughter, D. "Early Intervention and Its Effects on Maternal and Child Development," *Monographs of the Society for Research in Child Development*, 1983, *48*(4, Serial No. 202).

Sloane, K. "The 'Families in Family Math' Research Project." Paper presented at a meeting of the American Academy for the Advancement of Science, San Francisco, January 1989a.

Sloane, K. "The 'Families in Family Math': A Cross-Cultural Study of Parents' Roles in Their Children's Mathematics Learning." Paper presented at the annual meeting of the American Educational Research Association, San Francisco, March 1989b.

Smith, P., Carrasco, A., and McDonald, P. "Marriage Dissolution and Remarriage," *Comparative Studies*, 1984, *34*, 1–94.

Snow, C. E. "Literacy and Language Relationships During the Preshool Years," *Harvard Educational Review*, 1983, *53*, 165–189.

Snow, R. E. "The Training of Intellectual Aptitude." In D. K. Detterman and R. J. Sternberg (eds.), *How and How Much Can Intelligence Be Increased*. Norwood, N.J.: Ablex, 1982.

Solomon, Z. P. "California's Policy on Parent Involvement: State Leadership for Local Initiatives," *Phi Delta Kappan*, 1991, *72*, 359–362.

Sprigle, H. A. *The Learning to Learn Teacher Education Program*. Jacksonville, Fla.: Learning to Learn School, 1974.

Stephens, M., and Carss, M. "Mathematics and Parents," *Australian Mathematics Teacher*, 1986, *42*, 12.

Sternberg, R. J. *Beyond IQ: A Triarchic Theory of Human Intelligence*. Hillsdale, N.J.: Erlbaum, 1985.

References 177

Stevens, J. H., Jr. "Parent Education Programs. What Determines Effectiveness?" *Young Children,* 1978, *33,* 59–65.

Stevenson, D. L., and Baker, D. P. "The Family-School Relation and the Child's School Performance." *Child Development,* 1987, *58,* 1348–1357.

Stodolsky, S., and Lesser, G. "Learning Patterns in the Disadvantaged," *Harvard Educational Review,* 1967, *37,* 546–593.

Sue, S., and Okazaki, S. "Asian-American Educational Achievements. A Phenomenon in Search of an Explanation," *American Psychologist,* 1990, *45,* 913–920.

Swap, S. M. *Schools Reaching Out and Success for All Children. Two Case Studies.* Boston: Institute for Responsive Education, 1990.

Tabah, L., and Sutter, J. "Le Niveau Intellectual des Enfants d'une Même Famille" [The intellectual level of children from the same family], *Annals of Human Genetics,* 1954, *19,* 120–150.

Thompson, R. A. "Infant Day Care: Concerns, Controversies, Choices." In J. V. Lerner and N. L. Galambos (eds.), *Employed Mothers and Their Children.* New York: Garland, 1991.

Thomson, G. H. "Intelligence and Family Size." In Scottish Council for Research in Education, *The Trend of Scottish Intelligence.* London: University of London Press, 1949.

Tizard, J., Shoefield, W., and Hewison, J. "Collaboration Between Teachers and Parents in Assisting Children's Reading," *British Journal of Educational Psychology,* 1982, *52,* 1–11.

Toomey, D. "Home-School Relations and Inequality in Education." Paper presented at the Conference on Education and the Family, Brigham Young University, February 1986.

U.S. Bureau of the Census. *Statistical Abstract of the United States: 1988.* (108th ed.) Washington, D.C.: Bureau of the Census, U.S. Department of Commerce, 1987.

van Leer Foundation. *The Parent as Prime Educator: Changing Patterns of Parenthood.* The Hague: van Leer Foundation, 1986.

van Leer Foundation. *Children at the Margin: A Challenge for Parents, Communities and Professionals.* The Hague: van Leer Foundation, 1988.

Vatter, M. "Intelligenz und Regionale Herkunft. Eine Langsschnittstudie im Kanton Bern" [Intelligence and regional origins: A longitudinal study in the canton of Bern]. In A. H. Watter (ed.), *Region und Socialisation [Locality and socialization].* Vol. 1. Stuttgart, Germany: Frommann-Holzboog, 1981.

Vygotsky, L. S. *Mind in Society: The Development of Higher Psychological Processes.* Edited by M. Cole, V. John-Steiner, S. Scribner, and E. Souberman. Cambridge, Mass.: Harvard University Press, 1978.

Wachs, T. D., and Gruen, G. *Early Experience and Human Development.* New York: Plenum, 1982.

Walberg, H. J. "Families as Partners in Educational Productivity," *Phi Delta Kappan,* 1984, *65,* 397–400.

Walberg, H. J., and Marjoribanks, K. "Differential Mental Abilities and Home Enviromment: A Canonical Analysis," *Developmental Psychology,* 1973, *9,* 363–368.

Walberg, H. J., and Marjoribanks, K. "Family Environment and Cognitive Development: Twelve Analytic Models," *Review of Educational Research,* 1976, *46,* 527–551.

Walberg, H. J., and Tsai, S. "Reading Achievement and Diminishing Returns to Time," *Journal of Educational Psychology,* 1984, *76,* 442–451.

Wallace, T., and Walberg, H. J. "Parental Partnerships for Learning," *International Journal of Educational Research,* 1991, *15,* 131–145.

Weiss, J. "The Identification and Measurement of Home Environmental Factors Related to Achievement, Motivation and Self-Esteem." In K. Marjoribanks (ed.), *Environments for Learning.* Windsor, England: NFER Publishing, 1974.

White, K. R. "The Relation Between Socioeconomic Status and Academic Achievement," *Psychological Bulletin,* 1982, *91,* 461–481.

White, K. R., Taylor, M. J., and Moss, V. D. "Does Research Support Claims About the Benefits of Involving Parents in Early Intervention Programs?" *Review of Educational Research,* 1992, *62,* 91–125.

Wickelgren, W. A. *Cognitive Psychology.* Englewood Cliffs, N.J.: Prentice-Hall, 1979.

Williams, T. "Abilities and Environments." In W. H. Sewell, R. M. Hauser, and D. L. Featherman (eds.), *Schooling and*

Achievement in American Society. New York: Academic Press, 1976.

Windham, D. M. *Internal Efficiency and the African School. Discussion Paper.* Washington, D.C.: World Bank, 1986.

Wolf, R. M. "The Identification and Measurement of Environmental Process Variables Related to Intelligence." Unpublished doctoral dissertation, University of Chicago, 1964.

Wolf, R. M. "The Measurement of Environments." In A. Anastasia (ed.), *Testing Problems in Perspective.* Washington, D.C.: American Council on Education, 1966.

Wood, D. *How Children Think and Learn.* Oxford, England: Blackwell, 1988.

World Bank, *World Development Report.* Washington, D.C.: World Bank, 1984.

World Bank. *World Development Report.* Washington, D.C.: World Bank, 1978–1987.

World Bank. *Education in Sub-Saharan Afria. Policies for Adjustments, Revitalization, and Expansion.* Washington, D.C.: World Bank. 1988.

World Declaration on Education for All and Framework for Action to Meet Basic Learning Needs. Adopted by the World Conference on Education for All, Meeting Basic Learning Needs. New York: UNICEF House, 1990.

Yi, Z. "Changes in Family Structure in China: A Simulation Study," *Population and Development Review,* 1986, *12,* 675–704.

Zablocki, B. D., and Kanter, R. M. "The Differentiation of Life-Styles," *Annual Review of Sociology,* 1976, *2,* 269–298.

Zajonc, R. B., and Bargh, J. "The Confluence Model: Parameter and Estimation for Six Divergent Data Sets on Family Factors and Intelligence," *Intelligence,* 1980, *4,* 349–362.

Zajonc, R. B., and Markus, G. B. "Birth Order and Intellectual Development," *Psychological Review,* 1975, *82,* 74–88.

Zajonc, R. B., Markus, H., and Markus, G. B. "The Birth Order Puzzle," *Journal of Personality and Social Psychology,* 1979, *37,* 1325–1341.

Zaslow, M. J., Rabinovich, B. A., and Suwalsky, J.T.D., "From Maternal Employment to Child Outcomes: Preexisting Group Differences and Moderating Variables." In J. V. Lerner and N. L. Galambos (eds.), *Employed Mothers and Their Children.* New York: Garland, 1991.

Zigler, E., and Berman, W. "Discerning the Future of Early Childhood Intervention," *American Psychologist,* 1983, *38,* 894–906.

Zigler, E., and Trickett, P. K. "IQ, Social Competence, and Evaluation of Early Childhood Intervention Programs," *American Psychologist,* 1978, *33,* 789–798.

◼ INDEX

181

186

Index